# LET THE RIVER RUN

*How God Used Ordinary People to Do Extraordinary Things*

Dan Scott, with Austin & Tiffany Cagle

This book is lovingly dedicated to the first generation of Christ Church, who, under the leadership of L.H. and Montelle Hardwick, took the time to build a life-giving community that has changed the world. Their vision lives.

# TABLE OF CONTENTS

# INTRODUCTION

*"There is a river, the streams whereof shall make glad
the city of God, the holy place of the tabernacles
of the most High."*

When Saint Luke told the story of Christ and the early days of the Church, he invited his readers to confirm the stories with those who had actually experienced them. The apostle Peter did the same, reminding his readers that there were many yet alive who had personally known Jesus.

"We did not follow cleverly devised fables," Peter said. "We were eyewitnesses."

Whenever possible, it is important to meet those who have molded history. A book may introduce a reader to a great idea, but it should also connect the reader to someone who has actually applied that idea to everyday life. World-changing ideas are better caught than taught.

A living succession, a chain of human beings who intentionally pass wisdom from one generation to the next, is as powerful as it is rare. It is a river that connects the people of the past, present, and future into a single community. To discover that river is to escape the limitations of one's own era. Few people find it. Fewer still plunge in to become a living part of its flow.

Abraham Lincoln found it, which is the reason he could present our country's core ideas with such authority. From his speeches and writings, we might easily believe that he once had lunch with Washington or was a pallbearer at Franklin's funeral. Of course, he did no such thing. The founding fathers were all dead by the time he was born. However, he had a living link with those who birthed our country.

In his term as a United States congressman, Lincoln became an apprentice of John Quincy Adams, who was our fifth president, as well as the son of our second president. As if that were not enough, Adam's mother, Abigail, could easily be called the mother of our country and he was mentored in political life by Thomas Jefferson. Because of this intimate contact with those who founded our country, John Quincy Adams embodied the very essence of American democracy. The river of American life flowed from the founding fathers through him. Then, it flowed from him into Lincoln and from Lincoln into the nation's future.

> • • •
> *Lincoln's words did not come across as something he had personally created but as something authentically connected to the soul of national life.*
> • • •

After leaving the White House, Adams had become a long-serving congressman. It was toward the end of his career that he took the time to mentor that one special young congressman and connect him to the living essence of American life Adams had known so intimately.

Years later, as President Lincoln led the country through the fires of the Civil War he spoke with the authority of a founding father because John Quincy Adams had "anointed" him to do so. Lincoln's words did not come across as something he had personally created but as something authentically connected to the soul of national life. His words were the founders' words adapted to a new generation. That's why they had that "certain sound" of authenticity.

The stories told in this book are modest compared to these examples from the Bible and American history. However, the principles that make intergenerational cooperation possible are the same. Transmitting wisdom and experience across time always requires a person willing to transmit it and a person willing to receive it. Both must meet at the river of thought and experience that flow from the past and into the future. That meeting is what constitutes the mentor-apprentice relationship.

Mentoring requires humility – of both mentor and apprentice. A mentor must not "hog the stage," sucking up the time and space required for younger leaders to emerge and grow. He must offer his experience (and demonstrate why it remains relevant) to those whom he believes will likely gain influence and power. He must trust the current of history to do the rest. He must understand that younger leaders are never "ready" to lead, that people learn to lead by actually leading. He must also accept the painful reality that older leaders are never ready to quit but must "quit" anyway. Of course, a good mentor doesn't ever quit. He merely steps back, as an intentional strategy for producing young leaders.

An apprentice must take the time to receive the wisdom that is offered. He or she must then apply that wisdom to the challenges and opportunities of his or her own era. Without a mentor, a young leader will spend his life learning lessons by experience that he might have mastered through instruction. He will spend too much time in the "school of hard knocks." A self-made leader thus runs the risk of running out of the time required to develop those higher understandings about life that might have otherwise helped him make a notable contribution to the world.

Lincoln, like so many of history's greatest leaders, found a giant's shoulder on which to stand. He did that by submitting his life for a season to a great mentor.

We offer the stories and lessons of this book to encourage older people to tell their stories. We offer them to help younger people grasp the principles that molded successful people a generation ago. Since most of these people are still living, and are accessible to those who want to learn, they can become an invaluable resource for those who wish to succeed in life.

So plunge in, let go of fear, and "let the river run!"

# A VISITOR BLOWS UP OUR DAM

In the spring of 1990, our church experienced an extraordinary season of grace.

We often call such a season a "revival," although that is an overused and ill-defined word. Revival usually implies a period of emotional unrest accompanied by unusual and perhaps supernatural signs. In retrospect, that is exactly what occurred at Christ Church Nashville, although that is obvious only in retrospect.

*• • •*
*Revival usually implies a period of emotional unrest accompanied by unusual and perhaps supernatural signs.*
*• • •*

Many of us were Pentecostal. We had been taught to expect – perhaps even to demand – things like tongues of fire and miraculous healing. What were we to say about the appearance of a sudden and unexpected new ability to manage ideas and finances?

For years, our senior pastor, L.H. Hardwick, had encouraged us to develop our gifts for service outside the church. A number of other teachers added their voices to his call for a deeper understanding of Christian stewardship. David Anderson and Edsel Charles, to mention two of these teachers, constantly called us to a more serious encounter with scripture. These two men could have hardly been more different from one another! That was another feature of our unusual season of grace. Ours was a gathering of different gifts and dispositions – and even different opinions – around the common goal of discovering and living out our purpose in God.

Christ Church was not a cookie factory, a place where a well oiled belt moves lumpy pieces of dough toward the machine that presses them into pastries of identical shapes and sizes. The motley collection of artists, businesspersons and blue collar workers who gathered at Christ Church each week would have run for their lives from such a church.

The only thing we had in common was a desire to live without wasting life. We wanted to make our lives count. We had talked about it for years and were hungry to actually do it!

The tipping point came one special week during missions conference.

We invited Loren Cunningham, founder of Youth with a Mission, to speak at the four day conference. Cunningham was scheduled to speak in the Sunday morning services and in special afternoon sessions the following three days.

We knew that Loren Cunningham was a big deal. He had given birth to the largest Christian missionary agency outside the Roman Catholic Church. We were honored to have him, and so we encouraged the people of our congregation to attend all of his sessions.

That's why I was so disappointed with the crowd that Monday.

"Why are there just a handful of people here?!" I thought as I looked around our nearly empty dining hall. As starting time approached, I counted about thirty people. Embarrassed, I introduced Loren and sat down.

Time has a funny way of editing memories but I recall Loren as very relaxed, as though grateful for an opportunity to just chat with friends instead of feeling pressured to preach.

If he was irritated about the size of crowd, he gave no indication of it. He just stood up and began to talk. (What he said verbatim is lost to history. What I share here is what I recall.)

*I have been excited about our time together,"* Loren began. *"I believe the Lord has led me to talk to you about money and stewardship. However, I confess I don't know exactly what I am going to say!*

> • • •
> *The core value of American culture is capitalism; an economic system based upon the acquisition, multiplication and use of capital.*
> • • •

(Hmmm, I thought I knew what he was going to say! He was about to give us a song and dance about needy people around the world, about how blessed we are, and about how we needed to become more engaged with the global cause of Christ. Then, he would tell us how his organization would be a good place to make an investment in the Kingdom of God.)

*I want to set everyone at ease,* Cunningham continued. *I am not going to talk much about giving. I just want to talk about the nature of money.*

(Evidently, Cunningham was not complying with my skepticism.)

*What is money?*

*How can we learn to become capable managers of money?*

*How do we turn our money over to the care of God?*

*I have considered these questions for some time and I think I am ready to share some of my conclusions.*

*Let's begin with this: The core value of American culture is capitalism; an economic system based upon the acquisition, multiplication and use of capital.*

10

"Great!" I thought. "We told people to come hear biblical teaching, and instead we get a lecture on economics. This is going to be a disaster! I'm going to have phone calls for weeks."

*If you are primarily a Charismatic, you probably believe that capital is literally a spirit that rules our culture. If you are not a Charismatic, you will no doubt interpret this idea metaphorically, which is how I intend it. Either way, try to listen to my rambling presentation with an open mind. See where it takes you. In the end, even if you disagree with my premise, or believe I have overstated my case, you will have gained some new insights into the meaning and use of money.*

*Let's begin by thinking about how money affects people.*

*A wealthy person usually experiences a sense of well-being from having (and knowing how to use) money. This is particularly true if he has been born into a family with long experience with money. He often manifests an unconscious assumption about his status in society and is at ease around power and influence.*

*A poor person, on the other hand, may feel shamed for not having obtained wealth. Just as wealth makes it possible to become educated and to associate with cultured people, poverty often hinders a person's cultivation of culture. The poor person may, for all these reasons, develop an aversion to events and relationships that expose his or her financial condition. Naturally, the poor person is often uneasy around those with power and influence.*

*Thus, both the wealthy and the poor tend to define themselves by how they relate to money.*

*I will go further: this sense of personal power and self-worth that money grants is difficult to obtain by any other way, at least in our country.*

I wondered how Loren knew what it felt like to be wealthy, and yet also what it felt like to be poor. I tried to remember if he had some amazing 'rags to riches' story, but he was continuing with his thoughts.

*Obviously, I have been describing how unconverted wealthy people and unconverted poor people form an identity around money. Christians cannot do that, at least as overtly.*

*When a person converts to Christ, God confronts these natural attitudes toward money. Having no other gods before God forces a person to deal with all of his idols, including money, if indeed he has treated money as a god.*

*Be careful though – I'm not going with all of this where you may think!*

*The Bible teaches us to respect money. Although it warns us against making money into a god, it also teaches us that God gives his people money (and other resources) and expects them to manage it responsibly. That is what we mean by stewardship: the responsible management of money and other resources. The Bible addresses this topic repeatedly, in both Old and New Testaments.*

At this point, Loren removed his jacket, folded it over a chair, and leaned on the small wooden podium. It felt as if I was back in college, listening to a professor. Unlike college, however, this teacher had the complete attention of the room. Some took notes while others seemed to stare unblinking while Loren spoke. Nobody was falling asleep, which I knew from experience was nothing short of miraculous!

### What is Economics?
*Before we look at biblical teaching about money, let's look at some of the ideas behind the world's financial philosophies about money. We call those philosophies*

12

*"economics," and they attempt to describe how finances move and behave (or ought to move and behave) within a society.*

*First, let's ask ourselves why people propose or embrace different theories about money. One factor in creating an economic theory is the economic condition of the one creating the theory. A person's perspective on the economy is highly dependent upon how it affects him or her.*

*Just as money grants power and status, a lack of money tends to breed resentment. The poor often feel powerless and anxious. The wealthy often feel empowered and confident. These two states encourage different attitudes and beliefs.*

*A person's perspective on the economy is highly dependent upon how it affects him or her.*

*Sooner or later, a smart person who is also poor is bound to notice that he or she is not less virtuous, less intelligent, less pious or less patriotic than the wealthy people he or she meets. Naturally, this poor man or woman, who may be working long hours for poor pay, will ask why this economic inequality exists. Furthermore, this inequality will seem unjust. When you are on the bottom of society, it is tempting to blame poverty on structural flaws in the economic system, even to think that the flaws are there on purpose.* 'Perhaps,' *the poor man thinks,* 'our class structure was intentionally structured to keep some people on the top and other people, like me, on the bottom.'

*For the unbeliever, this line of reasoning may lead a poor person to hunger for some sort of revolution. He begins to long for a time of judgment, when the wicked people who oppress the poor will be stopped and economic justice will bring relief to those who suffer.*

13

*If the poor person trying to understand inequality is a Christian, he will probably not believe that a revolution would make things right. His faith teaches him that all people are sinful, so a revolution will only turn the culture's class structure upside down. Yesterday's oppressors will simply become today's victims. Therefore, a poor Christian may conclude, the wealthy are obsessed with money because they are unregenerate. They are idolaters who have been trapped by the deceitfulness of riches. They need to be saved and then delivered of their money.*

* * *

*In a world without God, the rich and the poor are always dancing partners!*

* * *

*The benefit of this sort of explanation is this: it no longer matters to the one who adopts it what others think about his economic situation. He knows privately that he is morally superior to those who are 'obsessed with money.' He can maintain his self-esteem even in the midst of his poverty. His interpretation for why economic inequality exists protects him from the shame he would otherwise experience.*

*Whether secular or religious then, poor people must explain to themselves why they are poor and must do so in ways that protect their sense of self-worth. Most people will understand this. However, the kinds of economic theories that arise from resentment will usually lead to a repudiation of those values and behaviors that create wealth. That harms everyone, rich or poor.*

*You probably were not surprised when I said that poor people tend to adopt those ideologies that protect their dignity. You may not have realized that rich people also adopt ideologies that protect their dignity. This is why wealthy people are usually more loyal to the financial system of which they are a part than are poor people. The wealthy will not*

14

*likely be receptive to the idea that poverty is a systemic flaw. Since the system works for them, they see little reason to challenge it. To them, their intelligence, values and hard work have paid off. That proves the system works. This belief may lead the wealthy to further conclude that poverty is the result of the laziness, ignorance, or dishonesty of poor people.*

*If this line of reasoning is correct, poor people's complaints are necessarily based upon envy.*

*Here we have the ageless conditions for class conflict.*

*It's like this:*

(Cunningham put his two hands together like a spider doing push-ups on a mirror. He then began moving them up and down.)

*In a world without God, the rich and the poor are always dancing partners!*

*The rich* (Cunningham wiggled his left hand, now underneath his right) *need the poor to do their work and to produce the products upon which their lives depend. Those who do the grunt work in industries like farming, transportation, construction and so forth help meet the basic needs of everyone in society. However, the poor also serve a psychological need for the wealthy, in that comparing themselves to poor people affirms that they have truly 'made it in the world.' Without this comparison, many wealthy people would have no point of reference to measure their success.*

*The poor* (Cunningham now wiggled his right hand over the left) *need the rich to fund the infrastructure that makes civilization possible – such as the arts, education, businesses and so forth. However, the poor also need the rich psychologically, because the wealthy serve as a natural scapegoat for poor people's frustration and resentment.*

15

*Because the world's economic theories arise from one side or another of this dance, they must necessarily take the side of either the rich or the poor. As a result, a secular economic theory seeks either to maintain the status quo or to overthrow it.*

*Here is what we need to understand as followers of Christ: secular economic theories are limited by the*

*The first order of financial business in a Christian's life is the spiritual condition of his or her heart.*

*worldview in which they are created. In a secular worldview there is no practical acknowledgement of God, of evil or of that invisible fountain of infinite resources we call "grace." Unredeemed people, whether rich or poor, live in a world where it is difficult to escape the pathetic dance between classes of people because there seems to be no alternative.*

*God, who loves both rich and the poor, wants to deliver us from that old dance. He wants to reconcile us one to another. To do this, He calls the rich and the poor into relationship with Him and through Him with one another. In the church, all earthly distinctions, all the ways we elevate ourselves over one another must be set aside and, by God's grace, gradually replaced by authentic relationships among them. As this occurs, abundance flows to all, supplying what is required to do everything God wants to do in the world through His people.*

### Bible Economics and Infinite Supply

*I am going to claim that the Bible presents a different view about money than any economic system proposed by the world. Furthermore, a believer's prosperity and productivity is not limited by the worldly system in which he or she lives!*

16

*Our success grows out of who we are in God, from what He has called us to be and to do, and from the faith that we learn to exercise in order to access His infinite resources to accomplish His purpose for our lives.*

*Therefore, the first order of financial business in a Christian's life is the spiritual condition of his or her heart.*

*Jesus calls both rich and poor to repentance. He tells us to lay aside our worldly beliefs about the role of money in our lives. He tells us that the poor, no less than the rich, are controlled by a "love of money." He insists that anxiety about tomorrow's provision is as sinful as obsessing about one's abundance.*

*In short, rich and poor alike must stop making money into a god.*

*Jesus also tells us to stop defining ourselves by how much we possess. One's identity can become a cause for accumulating wealth but must not become the fruit of wealth. In other words, we may become wealthy because we have been called to do something that requires wealth. We must not seek to become wealthy because we believe wealth will make us into someone important.*

*The right attitude toward wealth will lead to a mature view of biblical stewardship. Therefore, the Bible speaks a lot about the danger of idolizing money.*

*Jesus tells wealthy people to stop using money to control others. Rich people must not think of themselves as superior to the poor. They must remember that life is brief and that riches are fleeting. Only he who does the will of God lives forever. A man who puts his trust in "the deceitfulness of riches" is a fool.*

*These are difficult things for a rich person to hear because they challenge his very identity. If a person defines who he is by how much he has, he will not become a godly*

17

*steward. Therefore, his wealth ceases to be a real asset to him. This was the case of the rich young ruler, whom Christ asked to give everything to the poor. The Lord loved that young man. He also knew that the young man was trapped by his wealth. His soul was more important to the Lord than his financial status. The Lord was not looking at the resources this man might bring to the cause; he was looking after the health of his soul.*

*So, are we to think that a Christian should be a communist or socialist, as some Christians seem to believe these days?*

*Is the gospel really on the side of the poor and against the rich?*

*No! That is a very simplistic and erroneous reading of the New Testament. A Marxist reading of the Bible disregards the spirit and even the letter of Holy Scripture.*

*As it turns out, the gospel also has strong words for the poor.*

*For example, Jesus tells poor people to stop coveting other people's wealth. He even tells poor people to be content with what they already have. It tells them to stop judging others, including the rich. So, no, the New Testament absolutely does not call for revolution or for a redistribution of wealth.*

*Christians must not try to bring the rich down, either through violence or by political means. Poor people must not hate the wealthy. Wealthy people are God's children, no less than the poor. If rich people worship wealth it is because they are caught in a trap. Therefore, godly people must love the wealthy, pray for their salvation, and show them kindness. Resentment simply has no place in the Christian's heart, even in the presence of injustice.*

18

So, is Christianity committed to preserving the status quo, as some other Christians now seem to say? Does God favor the rich over the poor? Is wealth necessarily a sign of God's favor? Is poverty necessarily a sign of God's displeasure?

No! The Bible doesn't teach these things either. This attitude is alien to the teachings of Jesus.

Jesus seeks neither to maintain the status quo nor to overthrow it; He seeks to change the human heart.

Jesus says that whether we are rich or poor, we all tend to revolve our lives around money. That makes our attitudes about money a spiritual trap. Somehow, we must learn to use money as a tool; learn to view it as our servant instead of our master.

> • • •
> *Somehow, we must learn to use money as a tool; learn to view it as our servant instead of our master.*
> • • •

In other words, the Lord wants us to put money in its place. He doesn't want the love of money to control our lives. He wants our love for Him to control our lives. He wants us to tell money where to go!

Christian stewardship is not about gaining wealth for wealth's sake. It's about managing and maximizing our resources to advance goodness, truth and beauty in the world. Biblical stewardship turns a person away from the worship of wealth but it also instructs the Christian not to disdain wealth. Indeed, God gives some believers wealth because He has called them to do something that requires wealth.

On the other hand, God calls some believers to simplicity.

For example, if God calls you to live among tribal people in the Amazon, building wealth may divert you from the time you need to learn a language and teach the people *who speak it about God. Why would you need to worry about stocks and interest rates living under a thatched roof?*

*If God calls you to build a hospital, even in that same Amazon village, you will need a lot of money.*

*Do you see the point? It is your vocation – your calling – that determines the amount of money you need.*

*So, how can we discern the financial path God has called us to walk?*

*It's quite simple!*

*Just ask yourself if you have a purpose for building wealth. If you believe God is calling you to build wealth, you should be able to tell yourself what the wealth is for.*

*Secondly, if God calls you to a life of financial simplicity, you will be truly content to live that way. So will your spouse, by the way. One who lives with little because God has called him or her to live that way, feels complete. Life seems full and successful, even if he or she lives under a thatched roof in the rain forest. A joyful man is one who is carrying out his deepest calling.*

*Be careful though: never use "simplicity" as an excuse for laziness and ignorance. We are all stewards. We are called to learn how God's world works. Even if you are called to live simply, you need to know how to manage the resources under your control.*

*Don't fall into the trap of spiritual pride because you live simply. If learning how to manage and expand one's resources would inevitably lead a person away from God, the Bible would not have spent as much ink as it did teaching us about money!*

*Remember: the Book of Proverbs and most the parables of Jesus are about managing our resources. We can hardly use our faith as an excuse for not learning how to manage money!*

20

I could hardly take in all of these life-altering thoughts about money and spiritual life. I knew that something was happening, something that would deeply change those listening, including myself. This would be great! The church would suddenly burst at the seams with resources! We could build bigger buildings and host more events! As I began to imagine my new office, Loren burst my bubble.

*The most important benefit a church gains from its entrepreneuring members is their problem-solving ability.*

### What Churches Should Do about Money

*As I told you, my reason for talking to you about money is not to raise funds! What I want to do is help you disciple those who are gifted at managing money. Most churches don't do that very well. They tend to either bleed the wealthy for their money or run the wealthy off with self-righteous attacks on their financial abilities.*

*Here's another difficult message; churches are not called to control wealth. Churches are called to lead God's people into worship and to make disciples. The Christians who attend those churches are called to manage wealth. Churches that try to control their people's talents and money usually lose both!*

*Churches should inspire their people to create and manage wealth in ways that serve God and humanity. However, if a church really wants to do this, it must resist the tendency to control people. For example, it is manipulative to teach about stewardship as a way to raise money for the church. It is also counterproductive, at least in the long run. A controlling church culture stifles creativity. Churches that inspire people to create and manage wealth will of course reap some of the benefits of the people's prosperity. However,*

21

*a church must focus upon caring for their people's souls. It must inspire their people's minds. Teaching about stewardship must come from this motivation; not from a desire to get the people's money.*

*The most important benefit a church gains from its entrepreneuring members is their problem-solving ability. So, don't ask your wealthy people for money; give them a problem to solve. Give them a passion to embrace! Offer them your unconditional love and a vision that excites them. The Lord will direct them as godly stewards of wealth, when and how to direct the money HE has chosen to place in their hands. The financial ability is their gift and calling after all, and it is they who will give an account before God as to how those resources have been used.*

### We Need to Talk About Money

*The Bible talks a lot about money. So should we!*

*We must recover biblical teaching about money because God's people are meant to be fruitful. The gospel is a message of health and healing for the whole person, and for all parts of society. Godly stewardship advances this redemptive work. We demonstrate through our godly stewardship and generosity that resources are infinite because they flow from a Creator who is not finished creating things!*

*The core of biblical stewardship is simply grace – the belief that there is abundance for everyone under the loving care of God.*

*This is where our views of money differ profoundly with secular economic theories.*

### Are Resources Scarce or Abundant?

*Most secular views of money are based on a belief in scarcity: the idea that there is only so much to go around.*

That view leads us to conclude that if one person accumulates a lot, others will be forced to accept little. God's economics, however, is based on a belief in abundance! Abundance is the idea that there is infinite wealth to be had because the source of wealth is not within the material world. A Christian believes that wealth comes from the spiritual world. Therefore, there is more than enough for everyone.

*• • •*
*The church must stop using the word "stewardship" as a code word for fund-raising.*
*• • •*

A Christian should be confident that he will have all he needs for accomplishing all God wants him to do. The issue is never the availability of wealth but obtaining the necessary faith and wisdom to access and manage wealth.

Jewish people have demonstrated this truth throughout the centuries. As they have applied the lessons of scripture to everyday life they have often become wealthy. In most centuries, Jews have even accumulated their wealth in adverse environments. As 'spiritual Israel,' the church should be the natural place for believers to learn how to discover, manage and multiply their resources. After all, we have the same Word from which to learn God's instruction about money as the Jews.

This means the church must stop using the word "stewardship" as a code word for fund-raising. Instead, we have to become serious about making finances a real part of our discipleship training. Churches must also live within their means. They must resist the temptation to use gimmicks and manipulation as a way to fund their mission around debt and scarcity. Furthermore, stewardship teaching can't be merely about tithing; it has to help expand the resources of those who tithe.

*Don't constantly look for ways to take money out of your people's pockets. Teach them how to put money into their pockets!*

*Here's a final word about stewardship. We need to be good stewards of our influence over the Lord's flock. A church must create the sort of organizational structure that encourages rather than discourages their people to risk, experiment and grow.*

*Let me say it once more: if Christ Church wants to increase its influence in the world, it must resist the tendency to control people. Rigid, controlling systems attract fearful and anxious people. Successful folks run away from such places. So, don't become one! Place visionaries rather than controllers in places of authority and influence. Take some risks! Trust God's people. Feed them with a vision. Inspire them. Then, let them go!*

*If you will teach these principles and release your people to live them, Christ Church will experience great growth and influence. Your community will become wealthy. It will become unbelievably creative. Of course, it will not always be orderly; it will, however, be fruitful!"*

Loren concluded, I prayed, and the service was over. The people were wide-eyed with excitement, fear, and the sense that something had shifted. It wasn't yet clear what had happened in the hearts of those present, but it was abundantly clear that God had showed up in the teaching of Loren Cunningham.

# THE RIVER STARTS FLOWING

Those who heard Loren teach were reeling. Even though I didn't have enough knowledge or experience to imagine all the implications, I was on fire. I wanted the entire congregation to hear Loren's message. I believed he had brought a word from God to us. We just had to find a way to grasp that word and apply it.

(If you skipped through last chapter, I plead with you to go back and read it slowly and thoughtfully. Grapple with the thoughts just as we did that night!)

I finally decided to preach a sermon based on Loren's lectures.

I called it, *Let the River Run.*

I took the title from Carly Simon's track in the movie *Working Girls.* Our choir opened up the service that morning singing it full blast!

"Let the river run, let all the dreamers wake the nations;

Come the new Jerusalem."

If you have never heard the Christ Church choir, you can only imagine the sound. The curtain rose. The stage exploded. The people were electrified.

Despite this rather shocking call to worship, it was a magical moment. It would transform countless lives. Everyone present that morning would remember it for years to come.

I began the sermon by reading the 46th Psalm, "There is a river whose streams make glad the city of God, The holy dwelling places of the Most High.[1]" I told our congregation how Loren had taught us about vocation, finances and management. I said that the Holy Spirit was telling us to not control or manipulate the people. We were simply inviting God to do through the people whatever He pleased. The Lord wanted His river to flow freely through our church and out into our city, our nation and our world. To allow Him to do this, our church, as an institution, would keep our operations lean and modest. It would be the people of the congregation who would birth the businesses and ministries to carry out God's mission in the city.

*The Lord wanted His river to flow freely through our church and out into our city, our nation and our world.*

When I finished, the choir again sang "let the river run, let all the dreamers wake the nations!"

When we gave the benediction, the people, as though frozen, remained in their pews. Finally Pastor Hardwick said, "Folks, we will return at 6:30 tonight. We will open up the microphones to hear what you believe the Spirit is saying to our church. The Lord has done something extraordinary today. We need to discern what He wants us to do."

Most of the time, the energy one experiences in a service like that is short-lived. People get excited and then return to normal, usually after eating lunch. To our amazement though, most of the people returned that night.

After a prayer and a song, people began to file to the microphones. One after another, they spoke passionately

---

[1] New English Bible

about their dreams for ministry, business and the radical church organization that Cunningham had proposed.

It went on like that for hours and hours. Normally, even pastors start to mentally beg people to stop talking, put the microphone down, because it is time to go home! Not this night, however. Each dream fueled others' courage and passion. It was well after 10:30 when people began to leave.

The following week, our church quickly entered a season of unbelievable creativity. The congregation birthed great ministries and businesses; some which have gone on to make a national and an international impact. For years, we kept our promise: we encouraged people to birth new ministries, we did not try to control what they birthed; and we worked to build community among them. The synergy created by all these people living out their purpose in community immediately lifted us to new levels of effectiveness. Pastor Hardwick used to laughingly claim that leading our church was like running in front of wild elephants. "From the sidelines it probably looks like leadership," he said, "but sometimes it is more like running fast to avoid getting trampled by your followers."

Alfred McCroskey openly committed *Bibles for Russia*, originally a ministry dedicated to taking Bibles into the Soviet Union, to plant 1,000 new congregations in Russia and the old Soviet Republics. (They reached their goal in 2010!)

Dave Ramsey decided to begin *Financial Peace University*, from his Sunday school class notes, "Life After Debt," and his experience working with people in the church facing financial difficulties.

Nancy Alcorn had already founded *Mercy Ministries*, a resident program for at-risk young women, in Monroe, Louisiana. L.H. Hardwick had invited her to Nashville and introduced her to the pastors of our city. Now she was ready

27

to build a beautiful, debt-free facility on the lot beside our church. After that, she went on to establish centers in a number of US cities and in other countries around the world. Thousands of young ladies struggling with abuse, pregnancies, anorexia, bulimia and other issues have graduated from Mercy Ministries and now live lives of freedom.

> *. . .*
> *Thousands of young ladies struggling with abuse, pregnancies, anorexia, bulimia and other issues have graduated from Mercy Ministries and now live lives of freedom.*
> *. . .*

Dan Miller established a revolutionary ministry based on his book, 48 Days to the Work You Love. He and his organization went on to help thousands discover their life's calling and to strategize about how to fund and organize what they believe to be their life's purpose.

These are only four of the best-known of the many ministries that exploded that week when the Spirit touched our church. However, Nashville is filled with corporations that trace their roots to that week.

For the next several years, our church "let the river run." Satisfied to be a hub of the enormous activity swirling around it, the church paid its relatively small staff to serve the lay people who really led our congregation. That was no small thing; we soon were hosting Sunday crowds of thirty-five hundred or so! Meanwhile, the church profited from the synergy created by dozens of the autonomous and self-sustaining groups that began moving through and around our campus. We deliberately avoided trying to control the affiliated ministries and businesses. We just preached, taught, networked and inspired our lay leaders. In turn, our people created, organized and fueled their dreams.

28

Ephesians chapter four was happening in our city!

The dam had burst during that missions conference. Now, we had to create some banks for the resulting flood.

God had used Loren to confirm the new direction the Spirit had been giving us; now we had to organize and implement the new ideas erupting from our congregation. We needed to weave together the many ministries springing up around the city into some kind of synergistic movement.

Long before that missions conference, our church teachers had been challenging us to make radical changes in our lives. Several of us had taken baby steps to enter into our life's calling. However, few had been able to imagine how money or management could become such important parts of our spiritual transformation. As our revival continued, a few principles began to root our excitement to everyday life. It was these principles that transformed a season of grace into the long-term centers of transformation that many of our businesses and ministries became. Those principles were basically these:

1. We must discover our personal calling in life.
2. We must know how to fund our calling by managing and multiplying our resources.
3. We must work out our calling within long-term and synergistic relationships.
4. We must not confuse influence with control.

Anyone can learn these principles, which means that our season of grace is repeatable. An ordinary group of believers can learn to produce wealth, create art, and perform all sorts of fulfilling work and, just as importantly, can create a healthy community to maintain them. In our case, the church as an institution no longer houses much of what I describe in this book. That is regrettable perhaps. However, we have maintained our spiritual community because that is what sustains and focuses individual productivity toward truly great and historic accomplishments.

In the years since the dam burst at Christ Church, teachings about how Christians should always be wealthy have been spreading through the American church. Those teachings have influenced churches around the world. Although this so called "prosperity gospel" has undoubtedly brought hope to many, it has often been biblically unbalanced. Many have come precariously close to teaching something the New Testament rebukes: "equating gain with godliness." For this reason, we have been reluctant to write about prosperity, entrepreneurship and management. We didn't want to add our voices to those who seem to say that God always makes those whom he loves rich. At least we don't want to imply that the word "rich" always must mean "having lots of money."

What we experienced was clearly an explosion of wealth and creativity. However, the ideological foundations for our surge of prosperity did not rest on the same premises that many prosperity teachers seem to advocate. For example, many of our most successful friends chose to live simply. They didn't believe wealth was evil, they merely saw it as a distraction from their calling. They were delighted that God was calling their friends to accumulate wealth; but they were called in another direction.

By basing the purpose for wealth upon one's vocation, it allowed those called to manage wealth to exercise their gifts without guilt. However, it allowed those who were called to do other things to also carry out their vocation without shame and/or resentment.

This approach to wealth has made it possible to maintain community among people of differing socioeconomic levels. It has also helped sustain a number of ministries created by the people who chose to live simply in order to carry out their calling. Their wealthy friends know them and believe in them and have continued to support their work through the years.

The church's developing theology of vocation and wealth management helped us make sense of all God was doing through us. Although we don't claim to have the final word on how Christians should relate to money, we believe that Loren's word to us many years ago is still a good guide, even in the global economy in which we now find ourselves.

For those who want to plunge in, the river is still running.

# TELLING MONEY WHERE TO FLOW

*Dave Ramsey and Financial Peace University*

In the nineteen eighties, American culture was removing the ceiling over anyone who wanted to pursue wealth. We suddenly had little patience for our grandparents' advice. They taught us to save and avoid debt. They said wealth was built deliberately and gradually. We wanted it all, and we wanted it NOW. Their advice suddenly seemed old-fashioned and restrictive.

The way to "get it all now" was to take big risks, leverage debt to the max and move as fast as one could. Those too cautious to do so were wimps, losers, and nobodies.

It was the day of "fake it till you make it" and "dress for success." People were routinely advised to cultivate an air of success by going into debt for expensive cars and clothes.

Dave Ramsey was a man of the eighties. He embodied the spirit of the decade in nearly every way.

Dave Ramsey wasn't a wimp. He certainly didn't intend to be a nobody. He intended to win.

In his book The Total Money Makeover, Dave briefly tells us how he lost a fortune in real estate in the late eighties. As he puts it, "I was good at real estate, but I was better at borrowing. I wasn't dishonest or incompetent." He maintained a good credit score and paid his bills on time. However, he was vulnerable to a bank option that he, like many others, never expected to apply to him: the bank's legal right to call a loan at any time. When the bank called in one of his significant loans, he found he was unable to pay. In his own words, "I was as lost as a ball in high weeds."

Dave is a college-educated man, well schooled in business and finances. Although he now teaches common sense values that we should have learned from our grandparents, Dave is knowledgeable about economic theories, accounting procedures and all the sorts of things we expect bankers, investors and other kinds of financial experts to know. However, that is precisely the point Dave now tries to teach us: many of the economic theories he learned in the university simply do not work. They are fascinating and sophisticated but are actually little more than impressive layers of words wrapped around an erroneous description of reality. Grandma was right! Our economic gurus have been wrong.

Dave knows this firsthand. He had made his financial choices according to all those erroneous theories and believed them all the way to that wall he hit called bankruptcy.

In The Total Money Makeover, Dave decries the chaos that results from "faking it until you make it," "borrowing your way to wealth," and "get rich quick." He ruthlessly attacks economic theories based on such beliefs, whether they are followed by individuals, businesses or nations.

As he went through bankruptcy, Dave began to go deeper into his faith. Unlike many however, he didn't seek faith merely for the comfort it offered, but for the instruction he now knew it contained. He was especially drawn to the Book of Proverbs and memorized its passages as he studied the implications with Edsel Charles and other teachers in our church.

Years later, Dave would become friends with Rabbi Daniel Lapin and promote the rabbi's book, <u>Thou Shall Prosper</u>. He would affirm then what he had already tentatively discovered: that Christians had been avoiding the clear teaching of scripture regarding stewardship, debt and spending. Like the rabbi says in his book, "Christians presumably have the same text as Jews, they should be enjoying the same sort of financial blessing."

*If we are not giving direction to our money, it is unlikely we are giving direction to other parts of our lives.*

One of Dave's great lines is that the first principle of money management is telling money where to go. That implies learning to control our own selves. If we are not giving direction to our money, it is unlikely we are giving direction to other parts of our lives.

Rabbi Lapin would say that we must "learn to ride our own donkey." (Well, he sort of says that, in slightly more colorful language.)

## To Manage Money Well,
## You Must Ride Your Own Donkey

You already know what the real heading of this section should be!

We couldn't do that of course. The downloaded version might not have made it past your computer firewall.

Why then did we want to call this section something so crass?

Those of you who were raised on the King James Version of the Bible will soon understand why we wanted to use the other word– you know, THAT other word. You might even remember giggling your way through Bible readings at church, or sermons about Balaam. If you remember watching *Blazing Saddles* and its famous church scene where the women faint because the preacher used that other word once too often, then you really know why we couldn't use the title we wanted.

So please don't faint. We'll use that word as many times as we must to drive home a very important spiritual lesson.

Unfortunately, in most Western languages now, the word "ass" means something other than "any of several hoofed mammals of the genus *Equus,* resembling and closely related to horses but having a smaller build and longer ears, and including the domesticated donkey."

The Hebrew language however, never uses the word "ass" in a vulgar way. That's not because the Bible is prudish. To the contrary, the Bible is more explicit than modern Christian literature or what you, dear readers, will probably tolerate.

For the ancient Hebrews, the ass was a respected beast of burden; an essential part of any productive household. Hebrew children had pet names for the animal, just as you have for the family dog.

The Hebrews also came to associate the ass as a symbol for human nature, which we must guide to make it productive. For the Hebrew, nature was not meant to be the boss. Nature shouldn't tell us what to do; we should manage and direct nature. This is a very different view than our contemporary way of thinking, in which nature is viewed as irresistible and uncontrollable.

When the prophet tells us that Messiah will come riding "on the foal of an ass," it is a picture of a man in control of his own nature; one who directs himself toward intentional goals.

When an ancient Hebrew heard that prophecy, he would have immediately thought about another biblical prophet, Balaam. As we discovered in *Blazing Saddles*, that was the foolish prophet in the Book of Numbers who never became wiser than the animal he was supposed to ride and guide. Therefore, despite his great supernatural gifts, we think of him as a buffoon. Unfortunately, his lack of self-control and personal discipline led to his utter failure.

* * *

*A blessing must not only be given; it must be received.*

* * *

Samson is another example of this biblical principle; that for spiritual gifts to be a blessing to the people of God, the person who manifests them must become a disciplined and mature human being. Otherwise, his spiritual gifts destroy him.

In previous centuries when a monk demonstrated extraordinary spiritual gifts, his abbot would assign him menial tasks. Otherwise, the monk's integrity might soon collapse under the weight of his powerful gifts. Samson had no such accountability. As a result, he never learned to ride his own donkey.

Perhaps the most powerful picture of this principle is how God speaks about Ishmael. When it became obvious that the covenant line would go through Abraham's other son, Isaac, Abraham prayed that God would bless Ishmael. So God promised to grant Abraham's request; Ishmael would be blessed. However, there was a problem with granting that blessing.

A blessing must not only be given; it must be received. God would bless Ishmael but Ishmael seemed incapable of receiving the blessing.

As the boy's mother left Abraham's household, an angel appeared to help her and her young son. The Lord gave her a message through the angel that Ishmael will become a great nation. However, the angel warns, "he will be a wild ass of a man. Every man's hand will be against him and his hand will be against every man."

Well, that seems harsh! Why would God call anyone an ass?

Remember though, this word is never used as a curse or an insult in the Bible. God's words represent merely an observation about Ishmael's character. There was something in him that would keep him from receiving God's blessing. He was too much of a "wild ass" to handle instruction or to manage his own unruly nature.

Because of our reaction to the word ass, we fail to pay attention to the word "wild." To have called Ishmael an ass might well have been meant as a compliment. In that ancient culture, it's possible to think that being called an ass would mean that one was reliable, hard working and gentle.

Ishmael however was not merely an ass; he was a "wild ass."

The image is of an undomesticated, uncontrollable and therefore unproductive person.

To be productive, the ass must be trainable; capable of being guided by something other than his wild, raw nature.

A wild ass insists upon remaining in uncultivated, crass nature. It is unrestrained; uncivilized. It cannot become a friend of children. It cannot become an essential part of a household. It is disconnected from an economy because it rejects any intentional cultivation.

The judgment God was making about Ishmael was this: if anyone tries to offer a wild ass a place in his family, the frightened animal will buck and run. The wild ass won't accept a yoke. That was Ishmael's spiritual condition.

Physically speaking, the wild ass is the same species as its domesticated cousin. It has all the potential to become something more than a wild, aimless animal kicking about in the desert. However, it prefers its wildness. It prefers its perpetual lack of commitment. It fights for its radical and untamed autonomy.

This is a picture of that sort of believer who professes Christ but who accepts no instruction, commits to no congregation and remains in spiritual infancy – uninformed and unformed by God's covenant principles. He bucks about from one place to the other. He wildly professes his relationship to God and his commitment to Christianity. He is Abraham's child. However, he is more like an Ishmaelite than like an Israelite.

A real son of Abraham is one who accepts the yoke. He doesn't buck. He doesn't remain wild and unformed. He submits himself to become a disciple. He allows his thoughts to be formed and molded by the heritage of covenant. He willingly and gratefully receives instruction and then applies it to his life.

A man or woman must actually submit himself or herself to receive covenant. This is not only something a teacher must offer; it is something a disciple must receive. A "wild ass" will not do that. Therefore, such a person cannot receive the blessing.

Isaac laid upon the altar, knowing his father might offer him up as a sacrifice. His ability to receive from the past and to prepare for the future was the quality God required to pass His covenant from one generation to another.

Although Ishmael strikes us as much more naturally powerful than Isaac, his nature would not be tamed.

Whatever he learned would not be passed on. Whatever had been learned before him would not be received. He was a one-generational person, with no regard for what came before or what came after him.

He was a wild ass.

In his preface to <u>Seven Habits of Highly Effective People</u>, Steven Covey talks about his research of American self-help literature. He read through tons of books and pamphlets written from the War of Independence to the decade in which he did his research, tracing the roots of self-help literature to writers like Benjamin Franklin and George Washington. Both of these founding fathers wrote lists of proverbs and principles by which they lived their lives. Their principles, in turn, came from ancient sources of wisdom, such as the Book of Proverbs.

Covey believes a shift occurred somewhere in American history. The self help literature moved away from offering advice about how to find and apply principles for successful living and became instructions about altering one's perception and promotion of self. In other words, the literature began to teach that if one could envision in his mind's eye that the money were already his, he would find a way to obtain it. If he could convince the world that his possession of money was inevitable –he would have already acquired it in some sense.

Covey does not deny the importance of perception and imagination for acquiring wealth. However, he reminds us that acquiring wealth and keeping it are two different things! He also says that how one acquires wealth determines whether that wealth will serve or destroy the one who acquires it. The how and the why one pursues wealth becomes vitally important in Covey's 'values-based' model of wealth acquisition. If one wants money because he wants money, then that money will – as all idols do – turn into a destructive force, not sometimes but always.

This is why Covey reminds us of what our ancestors taught: that we should look at "why" and "how" before we decide to accumulate wealth. Knowing the "how" and the "why" will form the habits and boundaries that control and direct wealth. In other words, the person who establishes why and how learns to "ride his own ass." Those who don't, turn into a Balaam, a person who never becomes wiser than the ass upon which he rides.

*We must take control of our own financial life and ride our own donkey.*

This is the essence of what Financial Peace University wants to teach us: we should learn to tell our money where to go. We should not be mindless subjects of King Debt, of marketers, or of our own runaway greed. We must be delivered from slavery. We must take control of our own financial life and ride our own donkey.

Dave Ramsey came into Christ Church whipped. He knew he had to find some way to train and direct his "donkey."

He did two essential things that helped him learn how to do that: He enrolled in a Sunday school class and began attending it faithfully. He was not merely an occasional visitor, he committed himself to be there every single Sunday.

He also volunteered as a youth leader.

He did not just show up to the youth program when he felt like it. He went whether he felt like it or not. As his friend, I can tell you that when he says that being true to one's word is an essential part of responsible management, Dave walks the walk as well as talks the talk. In the area of stewardship, he has earned the right to teach us how to manage self as a way of learning how to manage wealth.

Dave learned to tell his money where to go because he learned to tell himself where to go. He's a good teacher and has what is probably a prophetic mandate to deliver God's people from financially slavery.

# CURRENCY REALLY IS A CURRENT

Mike Hardwick was nearly bankrupt in 1988. While in his thirties, Mike had been mentored by a highly respected Nashville investor named Dick Freeman. As a result, Mike had become accustomed to making very good money, mostly through property investments. All of this came to an abrupt end, however, because of the dramatic changes in the laws regulating such investments. Mike's bright new world had collapsed around his ears. He was depressed and disillusioned, and there seemed to be no way forward.

One morning, he had breakfast with his old friend, Mike Ballard. They met at Pargo's in Brentwood, and Hardwick shared his story of sorrow and woe.

Ballard listened and smoked, smoked and listened.

"When I finished my story," Mike said, "Ballard's ash tray was full and I was empty.

Ballard didn't say very much but he propped himself up on his elbows, leaned over our table and said, 'Hardwick, you know your problem? You've lost faith in God.'

I replied with something like, 'Oh, I don't think so. I still have faith in God; but inside I was fuming! What right did he have to say that to me? I went to church regularly. He didn't. What did he know about God? What in the world was he thinking? Pretty insensitive, that's for sure.

Late that night, about midnight, his words really sunk in. I had been trying to read a sports article in the newspaper.

When I put the paper down, I realized that I had not grasped one thing in that article. So, I read it again.

Still nothing.

I picked up my Bible and read a passage.

Nothing. I just couldn't focus.

Then I prayed.

Dear God, I don't understand why Mike Ballard thought that about me. I haven't lost faith in You.

But even as I said the words, God began to show me how I had gradually and unwittingly replaced Him with other things -- business knowledge, faith in my mentors, faith in my own understanding of finances – many good and interesting things.

He's right, isn't he Lord? I prayed.

Yeah, he was right, I said quickly.

So I repented. I asked God to forgive me for making idols of my business, my money and my mentors. I realized that everything had been His work. He had given and He had allowed it to be taken away and whatever happened next would have to be about following Him.

A few days later, an idea came to me. In retrospect, it didn't make a bit of sense.

WHY DON'T YOU START A BANK?

Looking back, that was such a crazy idea! What did I know about starting a bank? But I figured that Williamson County needed a new bank, a local bank, a bank run by people that local folks knew.

I talked the idea over with my good friend, Ed Richey. He liked the idea and so we began meeting with other friends and possible investors.

You can't imagine all that is involved in starting a bank. It's nearly impossible! There are several different regulatory agencies overseeing bank businesses, four of which had oversight on our new bank venture alone. The funding, the red tape, the paper work – it's really amazing how we pulled it all together.

I was teaching a Sunday school class at the time based on Douglas Sherman's book, Your Work Matters to God. The main idea in that book is that every Christian is in 'full time ministry.' I mean, if every time a Christian really 'sells out to God' he or she leaves the business or entertainment world in order to start a church or become a missionary to some exotic place, who is going to build bridges or do brain surgery?

*Everyone needs to know what they are good at and what they are not good at.*

The book convinced me that I was called to manage money and that it could be a noble and godly work.

Anyway, the bank took off and soon I was helping to run it.

Now, the everyday business of running a bank is really different than starting a bank. I was executive vice-president, janitor, mortgage officer, teller – whatever I needed to be. But it didn't take long for me to get bored.

Everyone needs to know what they are good at and what they are not good at. I can start things. I like the adventure of getting things going. I don't do well with long stretches of protocol and maintenance. And I really, really don't like overseeing employees. You know, trying to figure out why someone in the office is mad at someone else because of some slight or oversight is something I hate.

So I decided to start a mortgage company. It would have two employees – me and someone to do the paperwork. That's how Churchill Mortgage Corporation began and that's how I meant for it to continue.

Two people wrecked my plan – Nancy Black and Dave Ramsey, both old friends and members of our church.

44

Dave Ramsey kept recommending my company on his show.

I had advertised our company on his radio program almost from the time it began. However, I had not been very nice about it. He had the idea to do a talk show about money but he had just come through his own personal bankruptcy.

'Why is anyone going to listen to you, Dave,' I asked him?

His answer was classic Dave Ramsey: "Gosh, Mike, I have more credibility than anyone around here to tell people what NOT to do!"

The rest is history. The radio program did well and Dave kept talking about my mortgage company on his show as his audience increased. As a result, I had more business than I could handle.

Nancy, as you know, is one the best realtors in the city. She sent me a lot of business too. One day she called to insist that I meet a young lady who was moving in from Florida and needed a job. I figured I should oblige her, as she was responsible for many of my new incoming clients. I didn't want to ignore Nancy, but I didn't want any more employees! I wanted a business that was large enough to make me enough money and still allow me to enjoy life.

Of course, I ended up hiring that young lady. Then, I hired some other employees because we kept growing and growing.

Today, we do a lot of business. Churchill Mortgage is well known here in Nashville. What people don't know is the amount of prayer and Christian life that goes on in our office.

I never call a prayer meeting. I think if the boss calls a prayer meeting, people feel obligated to go. But whenever there are personal needs or business issues, someone will often call a prayer session in their office. You might be surprised to learn that most of the people participate.

My story has a bottom line, and it is this: something very powerful occurred in our lives during that season, and it continues to bear fruit in all our lives today. I am grateful to have been one of the people who was touched by the faith and fellowship that lifted us to these places of responsibility and blessing."

Mike Hardwick, like many wealthy people, learned how to use money only after losing his fear of it. He discovered that money was not a thing, but rather a force and a flow.

This is, after all, why money is called "currency"; a word that originally meant "water in motion." After the discovery of electricity, the word was also used to describe the movement of electric power from one place to another. In either case, currency is not a "thing." It is a force.

## Money is Not a Thing

Think a moment about that curious old expression; "Money is no object!" It's one of those strange sayings people repeat because they think it has profound meaning. Actually, like a lot of other sayings, the phrase has no meaning at all; at least if we take it literally. We use the saying to show off; to let others know that we want something so badly that mere money will simply not be allowed to stand in our way. Of course, we rarely mean it even then. At some point, money will always become 'an object,' if for no other reason than the fact that we don't have enough of it to pay for everything we want!

In a way though, the saying, 'money is no object,' is profoundly true. Whenever money becomes merely an object, most of its value fades. A paper bill from a government that has gone out of power, for example, is usually worth the price of a piece of paper! So, money may be an object but it cannot be a *mere* object.

The old saying probably made more sense to our ancestors. They were used to the idea that a physical object can carry a spiritual significance far beyond its material composition. To our Christian ancestors, bread and wine, although common material objects they used in their everyday life; could, under certain conditions, connect souls to unseen forces. Our ancestors' custom of using objects to do spiritual business heavily influenced their language and view of life.

Think about the phrase ministers often use in weddings: 'with this ring I thee wed.' Earlier generations believed that a wedding band could become more than a mere piece of gold simply by acknowledging its deeper significance in a sacred ceremony! In the same way, our ancestors saluted their flag as something much more than a piece of cloth. Clearly then, our ancestors thought that some objects were more than things; that given the right conditions they could cease to be "mere" objects and become conduits of an invisible flow of power.

We still realize that some objects are not "mere objects." For example, we all know that it is not healthy to stomp on a picture of our spouse! If you ever do that, I will assure you that saying, "but it was just a piece of paper, dear" will not atone for your offense! A picture may indeed be a piece of paper, but the little dots of ink on that paper turn it into something much more than what its material composition would suggest.

Money – like wedding rings, flags and pictures – is much more than an object. To prove that, try to pay a person in German Notgeld signed by Kaiser Wilhelm. For that matter, try using money backed by the treasury of the Confederate States of America. If neither of these works, try offering a person clam shells, beaver fur or a solemn pledge in front of three witnesses while you grab your groin (which is what the word "testimony" originally meant!) None of these units of exchange will probably get you anywhere, even though all of them have been used as legitimate forms of money at other times and in other places.

*Money - like wedding rings, flags and pictures - is much more than an object.*

A coin, a paper bill or a check signed by a person with a good reputation are all means of economic exchange. However, the coin, the paper bill and the check must bear important bits of information to give it legitimacy. If and when a society changes its opinion about what constitutes a legitimate symbol of economic exchange, coins, bills and checks can immediately lose their value. So although currency is usually an object of some sort, it channels a current, and the current is not an object.

As we mentioned, the word "current" originally referred to water in motion. A channel was either a natural or man-made means through which the current flowed. Currency then (in the economic sense) is the visible channel through which economic power flows, a material manifestation of an invisible power. The financial current that flows through human society is invisible because it is a spiritual force. It therefore requires a material "interface" to allow human beings – material creatures – to see and manage it.

48

(If any of you took me seriously and stomped on a picture of your spouse in order to better understand my point, I urge you to take this book and go read somewhere quietly while your spouse cools off!)

When human beings agree together about how to use financial power they create an "economy." (That's another word with ancient roots. It originally meant "to manage a household.")

Therefore, we can conclude that though money is a power represented by objects, it is not synonymous with these objects. The objects merely allow us to make a connection with financial power. Hence: money really isn't an object! It really is a current. That's why we call it currency.

All this implies that when we are dealing with money, we are handling a spiritual reality. Therefore, learning to be financially responsible is about learning how to deal responsibly with the spiritual world. For that reason, the Bible repeatedly tells us that money – like electricity, firearms, sex and wine are dangerous things. If we don't learn how to use them, they will curse instead of bless us.

Most of us are probably in a better position to understand this than our ancestors were (although we usually don't). We, of all generations, should know that money is no object. Our national currencies change their values daily. The Yen is up today; the Euro is holding steady; the Dollar is in decline. Tomorrow the scene may change. Thus, investors move their funds from one currency – or from one economic system - to another. As their opinions about the stability and strength of nations change, so does their faith in the respective values of the currencies of those nations. Furthermore, as time passes, all the world's various currencies are flowing into that one mighty economic Amazon we call the global economy. This would have astounded even our grandparents; it would have seemed utterly bewildering to our more distant ancestors.

To view money as a mere object seriously restricts a person's ability to deal imaginatively with financial matters. If one is restricted to thinking about "money" as merely a collection of dollar bills and coins, he touches only the tip of an iceberg. Such a person is unaware that the tip he holds is connected to a massive body that can shift and turn in ways far beyond his ability to predict or control.

## How Non-financial Conditions Affect Money

Think about it this way: wouldn't you think twice about entering into a long-term business arrangement with a man who is seriously ill? Sure you would; especially if the business depended upon the abilities of the sick man. You would hesitate even if you knew the sick man to be entirely honest. You would know that even though he has good character and excellent intentions, he lacks the ability to carry those intentions out. Therefore, we must conclude, sickness can affect economy.

A poor person who demonstrates some extraordinary talent may suddenly attract great amounts of money simply because some investor decides that his or her future looks bright. Therefore, talent can also affect economy.

One will soon discover that every part of human life is connected to, influenced by and constantly influences the economy. As you will recall, the word "economy" derives from the Greek word "oikos," or "household." As anyone who has ever lived in a household knows, everything that affects one part of a family sooner or later affects all parts of it. The nation's economy is no different than the economy of your household – just larger! This is also true of your church or business. Finances reflect, as much they control, the various parts of a society.

Coins make the economic current that flows from one part of society to another, visible and manageable. However, that economic current is generated by – and modified by · all the conditions of every individual to which that currency is connected. Thus, the value of currency is constantly shifting because the conditions of a society are in constant motion.

*Finances reflect, as much they control, the various parts of a society.*

A person like Mike Hardwick or Dave Ramsey is no different than anyone else except that they have discovered the way financial currents move. They have discovered that money is not a thing.

A piece of art, the promise of a trustworthy person, a stock certificate in a solid company, a parcel of land, and of course coins, are all conduits of economic power. As with the wires and switches that conduct electricity, conduits of economic current must be respected. However, financial symbols do not really have any power in and of themselves.

## Financial Idolatry

We can become sentimentally attached to a piece of land Grandma gave us, or to our first earned dollar, or to the promise of a friend. However, when we become sentimentally attached to such things, we must remember that what we have done is assign to those things a greater value than what the community at large is willing to acknowledge. Another way of saying that is, the value we personally assign to an object can differ from its "market value." We have the right to place as high a value on an object as we wish, as long as we intend to keep that object for ourselves. However, we

51

sometimes make serious economic mistakes by forgetting to distinguish between our personal value for an object and its market value. What we wish were true is not always true. What we judge as valuable may not strike others the same way. Money is not a thing. Value is not a concrete reality. Money is a symbol. The value society assigns to that symbol is continually shifting.

My daughter and son-in-law discovered this painful reality when their house burned last year. As they sorted through their charred belongings, they had to write down each individual item and assign it a financial worth. The insurance company was to reimburse them for their loss. To their dismay, the cost of replacing their wedding pictures wasn't what they had in mind! After all, they were just printed paper, and were worth only a few dollars. You can put a price on an object, but that price doesn't always reflect the value.

Giving a symbol too much respect (just as giving it too little respect) causes a lot of problems. Spiritually speaking, we call the error of giving an object too much respect, "idolatry."

Jesus told a story about a man who suffered financially because he committed this very error. The man had buried his bars of silver in the ground instead of taking a calculated risk to trade it in the marketplace. The man did that because he wanted to protect the silver bars. What he actually did was mistake a financial symbol for the economic reality for which the silver stood. As a result, he lost the true meaning of both the symbol and the reality. For him, money was an object. Because he believed this way, the object he so valued lost its ability to connect to the greater economy. By respecting the symbol too much, he caused the symbol to become a mere object. That's why he lost everything.

### Failing to Respect Money

It is also possible to commit the opposite error, of failing to respect a symbol. When we do that, we end up disrespecting the reality for which the symbol stands.

The Greek word for symbol means "thrown together." That implies that when a visible object begins to represent a spiritual force, our attitudes toward that symbol will affect our relationship with that for which the symbol stands. If a symbol is to be useful at all, something invisible must pierce through it and affect the person who handles it. Any believer knows that a cross is more than two pieces of wood; any Jew knows that a swastika is more than crooked lines. To respect or disrespect these symbols too much is to misunderstand (and perhaps misuse) the realities for which they stand.

Let's put this somewhat meaty idea into more concrete terms.

Jesus often told stories about farming to teach spiritual lessons. The reason he did this was that the same God made both the spiritual and the material world.

You will recall that the first line of the Nicene Creed says – "I believe in one God, the Father Almighty, Maker of heaven and earth, and of all things visible and invisible." The creed implies that the spiritual world operates similarly to the material world. That means that we learn how to deal with unseen spiritual forces by observing the part of God's creation that we can see and touch. Authentic spiritual life – including finances – is intimately related to the same pattern God used to create the material world. Therefore, a financial investor must have "good seed," "good soil" and a thorough knowledge about the right time to "sow" or to "harvest."

Jesus taught us about spiritual life by using examples from agriculture because farmers make a living by working with the forces of nature. For much of the year, farmers must work in faith that something is happening in a part of the world they cannot see. Their labor is subject to forces they cannot control. Therefore, a farmer must discern when to plow, where to plant and how to nourish his unseen asset. If a farmer digs up his investment to check on its progress, he will abort the harvest. Obviously, knowledge about soil, weather, seasonal change – as well as a developed intuition and trust in the created order - are all very important farming skills, and work together to create the expertise of such a worker.

All of these things relate to the entrepreneur or the investor.

Seed, soil, the weather and location are all vital factors in agriculture. Seed is only potential. Without it though, the process that moves something from "potential" to "profit" does not even begin. Quality of soil is another consideration; a farmer must put seed (that is to say "potential") into the soil. When he does that, he must leave the seed alone for a long time. He has to trust that the soil in which he has planted the seed will be good. He also has to choose a proper location, because even an experienced rice farmer won't do well in Arizona or Labrador. Oranges don't grow in Alaska. Time and location are thus crucial factors in farming.

Farming, in other words, involves many intangible and abstract factors. It is hard work but it requires intelligence and wisdom to guide the hard work.

This is true of every occupation, including those that deal mostly with abstract and invisible resources. That's why Jesus spent so much time talking about farming. If we can understand farming, we can understand anything because agriculture is the most basic human occupation. Agriculture is, quite literally, the first and most important "culture."

The farmer knows that there is a world under our feet. All the life-forms, root systems, tunnels and habitats, minerals and even streams of water create an underground universe that affects everything we do. Without that underground universe, the world above the ground would collapse. Jesus wanted us to know that this is precisely the way the spiritual world works too.

Mike Hardwick learned this lesson the day Mike Ballard told him he had lost his faith in God. He learned that the spiritual world – including our thoughts, concepts, ideas, attitudes and philosophies – exist in the "ground" from which all financial realities grow. He discovered that the symbolic conduit of economic power – currency - is useless apart from the connections it makes between us and the "ground": our spiritual lives.

Mike had no money the day he decided to start a bank. However, he connected to the current that creates money. He lifted his eyes above his situation – something often difficult to do – and looked into the unseen world for the answer to his lack.

A bank was birthed that night as Mike knelt to pray. But first he had to repent. And what was he repenting of if not idolatry, the old sin of looking at an object instead of through that object to things that really matter?

# A RUSSIAN RIVER FLOWS THROUGH

*How God Globalized Christ Church*

When the phone rang that February morning in 1988, I was in the church basement. We had five phones. Unless Lou was there to take the calls and direct them to our other eight church employees, the phones all rang at once.

Lou Hughes was our church secretary, office manager, human resources officer, head of maintenance and receptionist. That morning, she was exceptionally busy. I knew that because I had been trying to chat with her between incoming calls.

As I waited for her to get off the phone and continue our terribly important discussion, the other line rang. She motioned for me to take the call, pointing me toward the church kitchen, about five steps from her door.

The woman on the line said her name was Wendy and that she attended a Presbyterian church in Atlanta. She also directed a children's choir. Then her words seemed to rush out of her mouth, one on top of each other, each statement not yet concluded before another one had taken its place.

"The Soviet government has invited our choir to visit," she said. "They want our kids to sing in Pioneer youth camps. Probably in some Orthodox Christian settings too. I have no experience with liturgical protocol or anything else connected to Russian Orthodoxy. I called Wheaton College and talked to their librarian. He told me that he had some papers there

56

written by an Evangelical pastor on Russian Orthodoxy. Your contact information was on those papers. I decided to call you."

"So, wanna go with us?"

"To Russia" I asked?

"Yeah. All over the Soviet Union. We'll be there for nearly two weeks. Wanna go?"

"I'll let you know right away," I replied.

"We need to know real quick," she said. There's a lot of paper work. Don't take too long. I need to know like this week!"

I had just hung up the phone when Pastor Hardwick came into the kitchen for a morning coffee fix. I told him about the call.

"My, my, my" he said, taking a sip of coffee while staring into his cup. Sounds like maybe the good Lord is up to something, Dan. Why don't you see if a couple more can go with you."

The rest happened very quickly.

In June, three other Christ Church leaders and I – Ed Richey, Dave Cavender and Rick Stewart – got on a plane and went to Germany. There we would meet Presbyterian children and teens from Atlanta and fly on to Moscow, the capital of the evil empire; subject of countless baby boomer nightmares and bad movies.

Although I had been raised in a missionary family, I had never had a desire to visit Russia. I had studied the Russian language because I love languages and had met some Russian believers in Paraguay. But go to Russia? Why?

As I flew to Moscow, I thought about how God had been hinting for months about a coming connection between Christ Church and Russia. I went over the amazing series of events that had already occurred to push us in this direction.

A few months before, I had been watching C-SPAN. It was a Saturday morning. I remember that because we had called a work day for the church. Every able bodied member in the congregation was supposed to come with their lawnmowers, brooms and mops. As I was getting ready to go join them, I watched a rerun of a special hearing that had occurred the previous week in the United States House of Representatives.

(Now, you might be a nerd if you watch reruns on C-SPAN!)

*She shocked everyone by claiming that ethnicity and spirituality would be the central forces that would finally dismantle the Soviet State.*

Suzanne Massie, author and Russian language specialist, had become President Reagan's advisor on Slavic Affairs. She was addressing a panel of congressmen about coming social shifts within the Soviet Union. She shocked everyone by claiming that ethnicity and spirituality would be the central forces that would finally dismantle the Soviet State. She claimed that Russia would become Russia again and that the Orthodox Church would play an influential leading role within a revived Russian nationalism.

I felt goose bumps; the sort that sometimes indicates a matter of spiritual significance. The feeling did not go away, even when various professionals and experts followed her speech with comments like, "wishful thinking" and "romantic."

When I got to church, I shared with Pastor Hardwick what I had just seen.

"Let's invite her here," he said. "I'll have Lou send an invitation this week."

(Lou claims that when the resurrection occurs, Pastor Hardwick will be waiting by her grave with something for her to do!)

Well, Lou sent the letter but Dr. Massie turned us down.

So Pastor Hardwick called the head of the Tennessee Democratic Party, an old family acquaintance. He asked Ms. Anabelle Clement to write Dr. Massie a letter, explaining that we were not a cult or anything. (She was Bob Clement's aunt, by the way, our former congressman and brother-in-law to Pastor and Montelle Hardwick.)

Evidently, Ms. Clement got through to Dr. Massie because we soon received a new letter. Dr. Massie said she would come, but only at such and such a time and would need this and that, all of which was probably too much of a bother for us. (In other words, she wasn't interested.)

We decided that this was a God-thing, so we complied with all her requests.

She came one Sunday evening in May of 1988. She addressed a full house. As it turned out, she liked us and we liked her!

The conversations after church were lively and fascinating. She gave us her reasons for expecting a religious revival throughout the Soviet Union and told us that we should go see for ourselves. I told her about my invitation from the Presbyterians in Atlanta and she encouraged me to go.

In the following weeks, I read her books and did all I knew to absorb her information.

It is important, I think, to follow a "hunch," as we did with Suzanne Massie, to see where it might lead. God often leads in strange ways. He may not reveal step five if we refuse to make step one. Although step one seems sometimes strange, trivial or a "waste of time" it is often the door that opens to an adventure with God. A burning bush that does not burn up, a dream that haunts and won't go away, or a "heart that feels strangely warmed," may be the very thing that leads a person or a group of people to the purpose for which they were created.

I paid attention to the impulse I felt that Saturday morning while watching C-SPAN. I shared my hunch with the man who was at the time my spiritual leader. He paid attention. He thought we should pursue the matter, to find out if God wanted us to do anything about what we had heard from Dr. Massie. He persisted until Dr. Massie answered us one way or another. We listened to her speak. We followed up what she said by reading the material she suggested.

Steps like these must be followed whenever there is a possibility that God is inviting one into some new adventure. Someday we may know how many great inventions, revivals, or cures for disease were lost simply because someone just ignored a hunch or didn't follow a leading to some conclusion.

I have ignored plenty of hunches. That is the ordinary human reaction to a new thought. Thankfully, I didn't ignore the one I felt that day I saw Dr. Massie on television.

Paying attention to a hunch is not the only component of an adventure though. I might have failed to share it with another person. Or, having shared it, backed away after encountering ridicule and mockery. Many ideas die that way. That's why we must abandon those communities that become accustomed to searching for and killing ideas. During our season of grace, Christ Church became extra-ordinarily open to hearing and encouraging new ideas. That's how ordinary people from ordinary backgrounds ended up doing such extraordinary things!

Anyway, I had finished my Masters degree in 1988. In a political science paper on the Soviet Union, I had ended one paper with this sentence:

"The cross that graces the roof of St. Basil's Cathedral will remain when the hammer and sickle is lowered for the last time."

My idea for the paper had been simply that Russia was still Russia and that the Soviet Union was an artificial nation created by intellectuals. If I was right, then the Russians, who had been mystics and sages for a thousand years, could not have changed that drastically in a mere seventy years!

My professor didn't agree.

"NONESENSE" he wrote in red ink. "CHRISTIANITY IS NO MORE A FORCE IN THE SOVIET UNION THAN COMMUNISM IS IN THE UNITED STATES. YOU GET A 'D' FOR YOUR NARROW MINDED AND POOR RESEARCHED PAPER!"

As the pilot announced we would soon be making our descent into Moscow, I became very excited. I would soon see that cross on St. Basil's!

But what if my professor had been right? What if Dr. Massie was simply a wishful thinking and romantic advisor to a conservative president? In that case, I was (as some Christians in Nashville thought) on a communist-inspired peacenik tour, hobnobbing with those who were still persecuting Christians.

I was glad Alfred McCroskey didn't think that.

If Alfred believed in me, I couldn't be communist!

Alfred McCroskey might have been the most right-winged, cold war, social conservative I had ever met. That was not certainly unusual for a spirit-filled Presbyterian Marine from Florence, Alabama who ran a Christian bookstore. Still, we had become unlikely allies.

61

It had happened in a missions conference in Marietta, Georgia nearly a year before. The conference had not been that exciting. That's why Alfred and I had gone for a cup of coffee. As we exchanged stories, he told me about how he had met Haralan Popov, the Bulgarian Christian leader who had spent thirteen years in prison. Popov's commitment to Christ had profoundly touched Alfred. When he had asked the Lord for grace to make a similar commitment, the Lord had moved him to take Bibles to the people of the Soviet Union.

*To fall in love with Russia seemed unpatriotic, liberal and anti-Christ.*

It was funny, really. Alfred McCroskey had always associated Russia with everything vile and wicked. To fall in love with Russia seemed unpatriotic, liberal and anti-Christ. Nonetheless, a deep love for the Russian people and Russian culture began to grow in his heart. He would cry as he talked about a land he had never seen and had always hated.

"Dan, I want to take a million Bibles into the Soviet Union before I die. I am already growing old. I don't know how to start. But I am going to move forward somehow."

Suddenly I just blurted out, "Move to Nashville, Alfred. Mobilize our church to help you."

"Well, why not," he said. "If I can talk Jean into it!"

So he had. He sold everything and moved to Nashville.

Our congregation immediately received him. Dr. Jim Fortner offered him a rental house. It had not rented anyway and Dr. Fortner was a pastor's son. He wanted to help. Soon, Pat and Garry Malone "took a liking" to Alfred and Jean. Pat ended up becoming his administrator (for the next 20 years!) We gave Alfred an office in our church with a phone. People gave money so the McCroskeys could eat. Noble Carson, our pastor's father-in-law, would slip a few dollars in Alfred's hands every service and share encouraging words about how the Lord was going to make a way. Humble people like that just kept giving and praying.

Because of the openness of God's people, Bibles For Russia was open for business.

Alfred would not actually go to Russia until September of 1988. So I beat him there. (Also, I didn't get arrested as he did; but he claims that was because he wasn't a friend of communists like evidently some pastors he knew were. Sometimes he has a bad attitude, especially when he gets arrested!)

As we were forming our friendship, neither Alfred nor I knew about the other steps the Sovereign God had already taken to connect the hearts of Christ Church with Russia. While he was preparing for his trip and I had agreed to accompany the children's choir to Russia, God had been preparing a Russian family to move to Nashville.

The Chernish family was Pentecostal. Both the father and grandfather had spent time in Siberia preaching the gospel and they wanted a new life for their children. They believed God was leading them to immigrate to the West. In the days of hope that came with the new administration of Mikhail Gorbachev, the Chernish family applied as religious refugees to the United States government.

I had no idea of this of course, as I landed on that airstrip in Moscow. I didn't know that a year from then we would be receiving the first family of what would soon become sixty-six Russian members of Christ Church. I did not know that Deneen Alexandrow, a young American Baptist woman of Ukrainian descent would soon be arriving in Nashville to lead musicians to Russia and that her ministry would ultimately include our own Christ Church Choir. I did not know that the granddaughter of the Soviet foreign minister, Eduard Shevardnadze, would come to our church in a traveling dance troop or that she would be accompanied by groups of personnel from the Soviet embassy in Washington. I did not know that Robert Schuller would ask our senior pastor to accompany him to Moscow. I did not know that we would ordain a young rock musician from Leningrad – soon to become St. Petersburg once again – or that Alfred McCroskey would help that young man become the first pastor of Christ Church St. Petersburg, Russia. I certainly didn't know that Alfred would go to the microphone on that magical night as God was raising up ministries all over our church and say the most preposterous thing he could think of –

"I intend to start 1,000 churches in the old Soviet Union."

To this day, he claims that I laughed when he said it!

Well, maybe I did. By the time he said it, Russians had been pouring into Christ Church. Christ Church people had been running to Russia. All of this had been occurring through the agency of several utterly non-related and uncoordinated ministries who were getting to know one another on the run, well after they had each launched their own respective efforts to bless the people of Russia. It would be holy chaos for years which would drive our administrative people nuts, keep us like gerbils on wheels running from one thing to the next, and leave us so transformed that we can hardly believe all that happened, even twenty-five years later.

The four of us on that trip with the children's choir certainly had an adventure! We took Bibles to believers all over the Soviet Union. We met Baptists, Adventists, Orthodox, and Jews. Once, in central Asia, we prayed for guidance until a mysterious taxi driver came from nowhere and took us to an unknown place and then abruptly drove off!

(There were believers there, we soon discovered.) We had a personal meeting with the Patriarch of Georgia, which prompted someone in an unmarked car to pick us up and ask lots of questions about how we had arranged the meeting. (We didn't know ourselves how or why the meeting had occurred!)It was ten days of bewildering events and mystifying meetings.

It is tempting to tell all the stories about that trip. However, the purpose of this chapter is to tell the story about what God was doing to thrust Christ Church out of its provincial and ethnically limited experience and into the global connections that would transform its spiritual life.

If God could do that for us, he can do it for anyone.


### Becoming Globalized

The people of Christ Church were readers and thinkers. They were not the kind of stereotypical wild-eyed fundamentalist/Pentecostals that people seem to love to read about or see in the movies. The church had been catechized by Rev. Patricia Gruits, a teacher as demanding as any mother superior. Our leaders and youth had gone through her catechism, grumbling and complaining all the way. However, Patricia Gruits was not merely insistent that one learn her doctrinal lessons; she expected her students to meet God and to receive some sort of marching orders from Him.

Gruits had been invited to Nashville by Pastor Hardwick, who, by the way, loved doctrinal discussions and informed conversation. He had once taken six years to preach through the Book of Romans! We had visits from rabbis, priests, preachers of every conceivable denomination, artists, political leaders and business leaders all the time. Hardwick loved conversation with each one over long dinners at exotic places like Red Boiling Springs and various catfish dives all over Middle Tennessee. Once, we even had the UN ambassador from Bosnia – a Muslim – to say a few words in our church. When he finished speaking, Pastor Hardwick asked for our elders – old time Pentecostals who shook people when they prayed – to anoint the ambassador and pray for him. Which they did, in tongues!

Despite all these rather exotic connections, it is safe to say that our church was not a missionary-minded congregation. Nashville had been a sleepy mid-South conventional town, noted for country music. Although often called the Athens of the South, the gap between our famous colleges and the local population was vast. People tended to come in two racial varieties; Black and White, which were segregated at nearly every level, especially when it came to church life. Society was strictly stratified, according to class and wealth. The sections of town clearly delineated these divisions. Asking where one lived was a polite request for the information required to categorize a person. As for other languages and nationalities, these were nearly non-existent in Nashville. It would be years before the wave of immigration from Latin America and other nations would so drastically alter our urban landscape. In fact, it would have been a stretch to label Nashville culture as urban. For most of its inhabitants, Nashville was a regional city with modest connections to the world.

Christ Church had begun as a small congregation of mostly blue collar Nashville workers. Salt of the earth folk, they had gradually educated themselves. Constant conversations about doctrine and spiritual life had opened a new generation in our church to the opportunities that the eighties would bring. Our older church leaders were forward thinking enough to encourage their young adults to join them

66

in leading the congregation into the future. While churches all around us ranted at all the changes in the world and worked overtime to keep their younger leaders out of places of influence, Christ Church had opened up to the future - full throttle.

Learning about the changes in other nations was not a part of the picture however, at least for many years. Our local church leaders were just now opening up to our own nation – moving their perspective beyond the border of the American South.

For all these reasons, the sudden connections with Russia hit our church like a ton of bricks.

For example, Bill Smithson was a contractor in our church. He had built homes all over Nashville and had trained his sons to follow him in that line of work. He was not, in any stretch of imagination internationally minded! However, when Pavel Chernish came to town, Bill learned that Pavel had been in jail for his faith and that he had construction skills. Soon, Pavel was working for Bill doing tile work in high

*While churches all around us ranted at all the changes in the world and worked overtime to keep their younger leaders out of places of influence, Christ Church had opened up to the future - full throttle.*

end homes with an artistic flourish that had not been seen here for generations. The two of them prayed, argued, fell out and made up over a span of twenty years. Once, Pavel even convinced Bill to make a trip to Azerbaijan with him to visit the churches and believers he had left behind.

If we told all the stories about the Russian connections alone they would make this book 900 pages long! The point of all the stories though is this: God decided to push our church into a global era. He did it abruptly, dramatically and thoroughly. Today, a visitor to Christ Church takes its international crowd for granted. The visitor would hardly believe how the people of this church moved so far, so quickly to adapt their church to meet the needs of a new century.

Lately, it has been Nepalese and Africans who have swarmed into our church. Doctors from China and business people from Laos join Hispanics from Latin America to worship. No one bats an eye. That is the personality of our church. But those who were here when it was otherwise, smile as we recall those days of grace that made this shift possible, and the unlikely people he used to do it!

The Russians came here, we went there, we became friends, some of our children married one another, and when it was all over we were globally-minded people with our eyes on the world. Some of the water that rushed through Christ Church flowed from Russia. That was altogether surprising, as adventures often are.

Slava Bogu!


## An International P.S.

Jerry and Cherry Meadows are the extremely successful owners of a multilevel marketing business. From the first day they established that business, they have been determined to keep the Lord at the center of things.

They came to Nashville in 1975. After attending several churches, trying to find one that fit, they found Christ Church in 1982.

"It was a modest size church in those days," Jerry says. "The people in the original group had deep ties with one another. If you sat in someone's accustomed seat, they would let you know! But there was just something here, something that was right for us."

"We knew that we were going to build a new building before pastor Hardwick announced it," Cherry adds. "The dream was in his eyes."

"Yeah," Jerry interjects, "this was the quality that the church had ... A person could dream. In fact, we were encouraged to dream."

"Our business was already solid. We were often out of town because we had gatherings for our business partners all over the country. But when we were in town, we were always here. The church fed us something."

Fighting tears, Jerry says "it was spiritual food. Our church served those who were out doing God's work. In every one of our business gatherings, we had a Sunday morning worship service. Many people came to the Lord in these meetings. But this church was feeding us as we did all of that."

"Oh, by the way, we were in those sessions Loren Cunningham taught in 1990," Cherry said. "We needed what he taught because God was about to push us into the international arena."

We were already going to Canada, of course. Then one weekend we found ourselves in Quebec. The thousand or so people who were there were all Catholic, so we invited a priest to come to lead the service.

Now here is where the Christ Church culture helped us. Pastor Hardwick had taught us to always focus on those things that unite Christians. Especially since we would only be in a place for a week at the most, it didn't make sense to stir up anything. Anyway, at the last minute our local leaders told us that the priest had called and couldn't make it. They asked if we wouldn't mind to just give a short devotional. So Jerry talked about how all believers should know Christ personally and if they wanted that, to come forward. Everyone did!"

"That became our pattern," Jerry said. "We would just assume that any and all Christians - or even non-Christians if they wanted - would accept a personal testimony about knowing God. Since we were not planting churches, we gave out Bibles and just stayed in touch.

That really worked well in Poland. The priests weren't mad at us. The devout Catholics helped us. Protestants were happy. It all worked."

"Even Jews come to our Sunday services, Cherry said. "We talk about Jesus, but in Europe especially, where religion is so disdained, the Jews appreciate the way we honor the scriptures and try to obey them in our everyday lives."

Pastor Hardwick especially helped us develop this approach, Jerry inserts. "He always told us that God saves people. We are not called to straighten people out or get into religious squabbles. We testify what God has done and form relationships."

"Yeah, but churches have started, Dan, lots of them," Cherry says. "When we first went to Australia, we could hardly find the churches. And the people seemed so depressed. Some would say things like 'Well, we're just the offspring of convicts.'"

I didn't know what to say at first. Then I remembered that Loren had taught that every nation has a God-ordained calling and that the world will not fulfill God's purposes until each and every nation is represented in His Kingdom. So I told the Australians that they had a unique destiny and purpose in God."

"The international part of our work has been, well, inconvenient," Jerry said. "Most of our trips have not been financially profitable. Most of the others have been only modestly profitable. But we were taught to serve. And, as the vision grew in this church for the world, we extended what we had learned here to reach the other peoples of the earth."

• • •

*"God did all of this, Dan. And he did it not through the church directly, but through the people of the church."*

• • •

"When we first went to Europe, we had our Sunday worship, just like here in North America. Six attended the worship that first time. A few months later, it grew to twelve. Then twenty-five. Then fifty. Six years later, we would have a hundred and fifty or so. But in that sixth year, the translators were late. It was in Germany so we couldn't begin without them. So we started the service pretty late.

As a result, the masses started to arrive to attend the leadership sessions and thought we had already begun. They got in on the last part of our worship. To my great surprise, they came forward at the end. So many came that we ran out of Bibles and a Dutch businessman volunteered to get Bibles for everyone in their own language. He did it too!"

"Let me tell you something that happened recently," Cherry said."I had been wondering if anything we had done in those meetings had produced anything of eternal significance. That week, an Australian man came to our house.

'Do you remember when you first went to Australia,' he asked? 'It was difficult for you to find any believers to stand with you. Well, I pastor a great church now and wanted to let you know that I started my walk with Christ by walking forward in one of your Sunday worship services. I wanted to say thanks.'"

"God did all of this, Dan. And he did it not through the church directly, but through the people of the church. And we never felt alone. As we have been doing our work, we have been aware of others in our church, like Dave Ramsey and Tommy and Becky Scott, and of all the rest of them who have just kept on living out this vision.

None of us knew how to make it happen. But it happened. It really happened.

Praise God!"

# GOING WITH THE FLOW

*Or How to Match Your Work*
*to Your Gifts and Purpose*

Morris Sheats had just concluded his sermon and had invited people forward to pray. He had been leading a seminar at Christ Church and was concluding the visit on a Sunday night by teaching about discovering one's spiritual gifts. Christ Church had about 200 people in 1982 and it was easy to assemble the entire congregation for special events.

Morris was neither a prophet nor evangelist. His ministry was primarily in the area of leadership and administration. Nonetheless, the Spirit was upon him as he looked at a newly married couple standing in front of him. Before he knew what was happening, he opened his mouth, pointed at the young couple and began to quote Isaiah 61:

"The Spirit of the Sovereign Lord is upon me, because the Lord has anointed me to preach the good news to the poor. He has sent me to bind up the brokenhearted, to proclaim freedom for the captives and release from the darkness for the prisoners, to proclaim the year of the Lord's favor and the day of vengeance of our God, to comfort all who mourn and provide for all those who grieve in Zion - to bestow upon them a crown of beauty instead of ashes, the oil of gladness instead of mourning, and a garment of praise instead of despair. They will be called oaks of righteousness, a planting of the Lord for the display of his splendor."

"Write that down," Morris instructed. "It is from the Lord specifically for you."

He then began to prophesy about Tommy and Becky's life and how God would mightily bless their future ministry. He spoke the Word with such confidence that no one there that night doubted that what he was saying was true. No one that is except Tommy and Becky Scott!

The Scotts were in their early twenties and were busy trying to establish careers for themselves. Tommy had become an electrician. Becky was already a registered nurse. They had been a part of Christ Church since they were children. Everyone knew that they had been teenage sweethearts, had married and were becoming pillars of the church. But missionaries?

As they meditated on the words they had heard, they knew that Morris had merely confirmed what they had felt while listening to a sermon several months before. That time the speaker had been Ivy Bhagouti, a pastor from Trinidad. As she spoke passionately about the need for workers in the Third World, Tommy and Becky had been deeply stirred.

Now they were perplexed. How would all of this come to pass? Had God really called them to live their lives in some faraway place? They began to pray for guidance.

It was not long before they met Patricia Gruits. After laying out their questions to her, she suggested that they go to Haiti for several weeks and serve a group of missionaries there. So that's what they did. Although that six-week trip was extremely difficult and in many ways unpleasant, it introduced them to what would become their lifelong ministry of serving Christian workers in all parts of the world.

Tommy and Becky's employers were sympathetic to their missionary call. However, they were reluctant to give them the amount of time the Scotts needed abroad. So Tommy began to feel strongly that they should put their trust in the Lord; that He would provide their needs - which by 1986 included two small children. After much prayer, Tommy told Becky that he intended to quit his job and begin his own business.

This would be a real step of faith because Becky had become a full time mom. Tommy's income provided all of their financial needs.

When Tommy told his boss about his plans, he said, "Tommy, you can be a successful missionary or you can be a successful electrical contractor. I don't think you can do both."

Tommy replied that he was confident that God would help him manage all he had been called to do. So with his employer's blessing, he left the company and set out on his own.

With their meager savings; but without a steady income, work vehicles, office space or customers, the Scotts established their new business on July 1, 1987.

They needed a new name for their company. What would it be? They finally settled on Anchor Electric because they had decided to anchor their future and fortune in God. The Lord quickly responded to their faith. Because their small home equity loan was approved, they were able to purchase a small used truck. Then, a major electrical equipment supplier offered to provide all of the material the Scotts would need to start their company and assured them that they could pay when the business began to make a profit.

In the meantime, licensure regulations required Tommy's old company to hire him in a consulting capacity.

They paid a monthly stipend for this service, which kept the Scott family fed and clothed.

Anchor Electric, which God Himself had called into existence, which had been dedicated to His service, was wholly dependent upon His provision. From the very first, God showed Himself faithful.

The Scotts did not allow the business to keep them from carrying out their missionary calling. They traveled, often with their young children, to Haiti, Mexico, South America, Eastern Europe, China, and any part of the world that had a need. They carried out their vision of serving Christian workers by building churches, providing clothes, shoes, medications, teaching materials and other supplies the workers needed to do their work.

*God was at work in this part of their journey just as he had been in the past.*

At one point, the Scotts decided to sell their home and business and go to the mission field full time. They listed the home and business and prepared to move. However, Jim Enoch told them that God would not be sending them abroad but rather would be using them from their current base in Nashville. They smiled and continued their preparations to move. However, no one ever came to see the house and no one was interested in the business. Confused, they took down the for-sale signs and returned to business as usual.

However, word of their mission had been spreading. They were now receiving offerings from corporations, ministries and individuals. They needed a way to give tax credits for these gifts and so they created a not-for-profit corporation: Haven Foundation. Although getting approval for not-for-profit entities can be a lengthy process, their request was approved in record time. God was at work in this part of their journey just as he had been in the past.

Anchor Electric had continued to grow. The small truck had been replaced with a fleet of vehicles. The company needed fifty employees to carry the work load.

The ministry also grew as demands came from all over the world. Donations poured in as well, unsolicited and rarely even expected. They were stuffing missions supplies into every available nook and cranny of their business.

On September 26, 1997, while working at her shop, Becky (not known for being a mystic or anything!) heard the voice of the Lord.

"Prepare me a place. I'm going to send you some stuff."

"He really said the word STUFF," Becky insists. "I don't hear from God everyday so I remember exactly what He said."

Not sure if this really was the Lord, Becky pondered the Word for a few days and didn't mention what she felt to Tommy.

A few days later, she heard the Lord say once again,

"Prepare me a place. I'm going to send you some stuff."

Now she went to Tommy and through tears told him what God had said.

They immediately began to search for a place. But where? Their shop and parking lot was all they had available.

Two days later, two parcels of property adjacent to their present property in Madison became available. They bought it. They immediately began construction on a 10,000 square feet warehouse, "preparing God a place." They finished it in November of 1998. True to his word, God began sending goods, people, and resources. Unsolicited, huge trucks full of clothing, shoes, medications, furniture and other kinds of supplies began to come from near and far.

Their on-the-job learning experience allowed them to build a reputation for running a highly ethical and competent missionary supply center. Their knowledge and expertise for gathering, packing, and shipping missions supplies has made them a much sought after resource in the missions community.

The Scott's ministry has continued to thrive. They can hardly remember how many duffle bags filled with medications that they have personally carried through customs of nations all over the world. They have lost count of the many wells they have dug, the buildings they have constructed, the teams they have led, and the smiles of delighted missionaries, doctors and pastors receiving the supplies. What they can count is the multitude of blessings they keep receiving and the friends they keep making, all over the globe.

### A Dan Miller Perspective

If Dave Ramsey represents our church's teaching about stewardship, Dan Miller represents our focus on vocation.

Vocation is an old word. It is rarely used now. Nonetheless, it expresses something valuable. An occupation is not the same thing as a vocation, although people tend to treat it as a more modern way of saying the same thing.

Occupation comes from Latin, and merely means "to be present in a particular place." That is an adequate definition for much modern work, to be sure.

Vocation also comes from Latin. It means "calling." The idea behind the word, "vocation" is that people enter certain lines of work because that was how they are wired.

God calls people to do what they do. Work, thus, flows out of the deepest part of a person's being.

Dan Miller thinks that so many of us are profoundly unhappy with our work because we are merely "occupying the space in which we do something to provide for ourselves." We do not feel called to do that work but feel that we have no choice. As a result, our work does not resonate with who we are. We are not doing what we feel designed to do.

The years go by as we occupy our occupation. No matter how much money we make from it; no matter how many times we tell ourselves that we should be grateful for it; we keep sensing that something about our life is simply not in harmony with the way we are wired.

Dan decided to spend the rest of his life helping people discover why they don't like their occupation. He wants to help people discover their vocation.

Like most people with a passionate cause, Dan stumbled upon his own vocation. Raised in a horse and buggy Mennonite household, he grew up believing that his father had entered the ministry because of social pressure and not because he had a deep sense of divine guidance. Dan had experienced his community as "stuck" in a past era, disconnected from the opportunities modern life offers; and without the internal freedom needed to choose from among those opportunities. Although he has the deepest respect for his father, he didn't intend to live his life that way.

The first step away from his religious community was Joanne. She was not Mennonite. She was not a farmer. Marrying her was a major break with the past.

Life was not always easy for them. Dan and Joanne experienced their share of challenges. By the time they came to Christ Church however, they knew that they had to worship within a community in which there was freedom to explore the world and to go on personal adventures. Fortunately, they came to the church just as it was bursting with just that sort of freedom.

He wrote <u>48 Days to the Work You Love</u> because he just had to share his belief that work is too important a part of life to merely occupy it. He likes to quote the statistics about how a huge percentage of heart attacks occur on Monday mornings. Great numbers of people simply hate their jobs.

The situation has gotten worse, unfortunately. Cartoons like Dilbert, and sitcoms like The Office, reveal that many Americans now view their jobs as barely tolerable.

* * *

*Dan believes that we stay in such situations because of internal, rather than an external control.*

* * *

Most of our grandparents worked in jobs that allowed them to decide when to take a break, or how hard to push themselves any given day. In contrast, much of our work is regulated to produce the maximum efficiency for the company that employs us. Add to that a boss without people skills or an environment without natural light, or any other freedom-robbing factors that erode our sense of human dignity, and it's no wonder we rate our jobs with death and taxes among the unavoidable tragedies of life.

Dan believes that we stay in such situations because of internal, rather than an external control. We think there is no alternative. Sometimes, for the short term, that may be the case. However, there is always a way out for the one willing to change his or her lifestyle, the place he lives or his level of education. If we can endure the displeasure of our loved ones; or worse still, our own internal shaming voices; we can find work that makes us want to get up in the morning and accomplish something. We can find work that matches the flow of our personality, passion, gifts, experience and disposition. Dan claims we can do it in 48 days!

As I listened to Tommy and Becky Scott's story, I thought about what Dan would say about their choices. First, he would note that they were willing to leave their security in search of fulfillment. Secondly, they were willing to listen and discern what God might be saying. Thirdly, they took concrete steps toward their future instead of "waiting on the Lord," to magically provide. Fourthly, they adapted their vision to what they were learning. Although they were willing to become full time missionaries, they widened their definition of "missionary" to include a corporate supply station for missions work. Fifthly, they did not slavishly follow the models of others; they started with the models of others and kept tweaking what they had learned until it suited their personalities and their circumstances. Finally, they kept on doing what they do, day after day, week after week, and year after year simply because they love it. It is who they are.

Dan would point out that history's saints are all very different one from another. The closer people get to God, the more they become who and what God created them uniquely to be. Abraham was not cloned. No one was ever like Moses. Mother Teresa was not Billy Graham. God likes variety and individuality. Goose-stepping displays of masses of people locked into a rhythm of conformity impresses the dark side. It is not for the people of God.

In the movie, Chariots of Fire, when the hero's sister reproaches him for going into sports because he had claimed a call to be a missionary, he replies "God HAS called me to be a missionary, and I will be one; but He also made me to run fast and when I run, I feel His pleasure."

That is Dan's message and he has pushed and prodded us all to learn it. Dan Miller just hates the idea that work is punishment; that somehow in a perfect world no one would work. he just doesn't resonate with the attitude of the Big Rock Candy Mountain:

"In the Big Rock Candy Mountains the jails are made of tin,
And you can walk right out again as soon as you are in.
There ain't no short-handled shovels, no axes, saws or picks,
I'm a-goin' to stay where you sleep all day
Where they hung the jerk that invented work
In the Big Rock Candy Mountain[2]"

Dan Miller would tell us that hanging "the jerk that invented work" is going to take a very big rope. According to Genesis, God was the one who invented work. Furthermore, work was not a punishment; Adam worked before he sinned and got kicked out of Eden! In fact, even God worked to create the world. Then on the seventh day, "He rested from His labors." So the Big Rock Candy Mountain promises something that even Eden couldn't deliver!

Of course, the fall changed everything, including the nature of work. There is no place on earth now where "there ain't no short-handled shovels, no axes, saws or picks," or where one can "stay where you sleep all day." If one avoids all short-handled shovels, axes, saws and picks" and only "stays where you sleep all day," he is going to be very poor! Someone, somewhere has to use instruments like the ones forbidden in the Big Rock Candy Mountain or there will be no food for us to eat. If someone is willing to do that work with such

---

[2] Billy Mack,1928, Denton & Haskins Music Pub. Co. Inc., 1595 Broadway, New York, N.Y.

instruments, the rest of us have to pay him for his work, pay someone else to transport it, pay someone else to package it, someone to tell us where to get it, and so forth. All the people who work together to get the food from the field to our tables create an economic system. However, every piece of the system relies on the "sweat of your brow," and all those nasty instruments like "short-handled shovels."

Dan Miller knows that some people are just wired to love digging with a shovel, others love to refine the minerals the worker discovers, others market the products made from those minerals – a vibrant social life requires people with diverse gifts and passions all doing what they love to do.

*The power of our church was the freedom we gave to one another to become all God had called us to be.*

Whether you can discover what you're wired for in 48 days or not, I'll leave to Dan Miller.

The issue for us is that the revival God sent to Christ Church was as much about discovering our personal calling as it was about managing our personal resources.

Tommy and Becky Scott are just two examples among thousands who kept inquiring of God and other people until they discovered the work they loved.

As an institution, Christ Church never had much of a vision. That was its greatness. The power of our church was the freedom we gave to one another to become all God had called us to be. The institution just kept us connected.

How many local churches have had missions departments that ever accomplished what Tommy and Becky have accomplished? And they are only one story out of dozens. Many of our people created agencies that have blessed the world in astounding ways. So what did our church missions department do? It introduced new people to our missions-minded folk. It enlisted volunteers for their agencies. It helped synchronize and synergize the work of the various people and agencies connected to the church. It had a conference once a year to showcase all that it had been doing and to educate the congregation about ways to get involved in the world-wide cause of Christ.

Christ Church at its best has encouraged people to become themselves. It has helped people stop resisting the natural flow of life that comes from who they are.

"So," someone may ask, "doesn't that approach just produce self-centered autonomous individuals and undermine community?"

My answer comes from a dark and painful moment in Tommy and Becky's lives.

One terrible night in February 2007, a group of us drove to their door in a snowstorm to tell them that their daughter had been killed with Eric Falk while they were on their way to a missions conference. Numb with disbelief, Tommy and Becky walked though the next few days preparing for the memorial service.

The day and night before that service, thousands of people filed past the bodies. Tommy and Becky stood there hour after hour, often comforting our grief-stricken people. Highly educated professors from the university waited in line for an hour or so with nurses and orderlies still in scrubs, custodians, bus drivers and nursery teachers. There were Hispanic bricklayers, Chinese students, and Iranian immigrants. There were old people in walkers and children with their parents. One after another, hour after hour they came. They wept, they laughed, and they hugged.

The funeral services were packed. People had come from everywhere. They came because they loved; because they were part of a community.

A community is not a cult. A healthy community helps people become what they most long to be. It celebrates the beautiful mosaic of a free and productive people who realize that what they are together is much more than merely the sum of the collective parts.

Tommy and Becky; Dan and Joanne. Not much in common except the grace to rejoice in how God has helped them to become exactly what He decided for them to be; long before He had ever formed a star. They have in common their belief that God makes us all unique and that we become most what He wants by becoming ourselves – by going with the flow of our deepest sense of self.

# A RIVER HAS BANKS

*How Administrative People Created Systems*
*to Keep the River Flowing*


In 1992, a group of Christ Church leaders met at St. Mary's Episcopal retreat center at Monteagle, Tennessee, to talk about how to provide spiritual direction and support for our emerging leaders. We wanted to follow the teaching of Ephesians four, which clearly instructs spiritual leaders to train believers to do the work of the ministry. We wanted to avoid the common church business trap of creating a staff to do the work of ministry.

The participants were Dan Scott, Don Wood, Beverly Robbins, Charles Oakes, and a few others whose names I have unfortunately forgotten. The meeting was creative and stormy! We all had strong feelings about the inadequacy and dysfunction of traditional church systems and we didn't want to perpetuate them. However, how would we minister to our growing congregation without expanding a church bureaucracy? Somehow, we had to separate "church as institution" from "church as body of Christ," without demonizing the institution or demoting the biblical role of administrative systems.

The problem as we saw it is that in a culture like ours, business values and structure tend to look like common sense for every aspect of life. For this reason, schools, clinics and churches - which must have administrative structures – tend to copy those structures from for-profit corporations. In many cases, that structure gradually erodes the core purpose unique to those entities.

The Old Testament story of David and Goliath illustrates how this works. Saul wanted to help David and so offered him the armor and weaponry that Saul understood. David knew, however, that armor was wrong for him. He was a slingshot sort of fighter. He needed mobility and flexibility. The armor, good for Saul, would cripple his gifts and lead to his defeat.

Applying the culture of a for-profit business to a non-profit organization is like dressing David in Saul's armor. For example, in a college, if few students are interested in learning astrophysics, a university committed to a for-profit model may drop astrophysics from its curriculum. The university will gradually organize around trendy and profit-making courses.

A church that does this may gradually lose the core purpose for its existence and dedicate itself to a model of never ending expansion of facilities and members. That, in turn, creates a climate in which the church is trapped in a cycle of ceaseless fund-raising to sustain its over-bloated sense of identity.

We were growing but we did not want to become a "McChurch." We wanted to develop our knowledge of God and scripture, deepen our connection to God, make a spiritual impact on culture, and make disciples. We especially wanted to be faithful to the word God had given us through Loren Cunningham.

How does a church develop administrative systems that support but do not control lay and pastoral leaders? That was the question before us.

The group was blessed with two administrative people who entered the conversation with a heart to serve: Donnie Wood and Beverly Robbins. Beverly would soon emerge as a gifted and called teacher, which we will note in another chapter. However, Donnie Wood was laser focused on this task of raising up lay structures of ministry and influence within our church. Along with our church administrator, David Cavender, Donnie would develop models that would thrust a huge percentage of our congregation into active service.

Donnie Wood grew up in Christ Church. In fact, when he was a boy, his father was once the church administrator. By the time this story begins, Donnie had already begun his own business, Don Wood Plumbing, which was well on its way to becoming a major business in its own right. So Donnie knew how to organize things. His wife, Cris, was also an entrepreuring person, full of energy and ready to serve our congregation.

When we realized that we needed a structure to provide pastoral care and spiritual formation – that mom and pop systems simply would no longer do the trick - Donnie and Cris seemed to be the right people to organize it. After Don and Cris met with Dan Scott, John Dyson and Lynn Husband several times, they went to work to envision a ministry called the Barnabas Ministry. The name was a reference to St. Barnabas the Encourager, St. Paul's first companion and mentor of John Mark, writer of the fourth gospel. The New Testament calls him, "the son of consolation." He was a priest, an unusual vocation in the early days of the church, and embodied in his vocation and demeanor what it means to love and pastor a flock. It was a good name for our work of raising up deacons, pastors and caregivers.

However, the name of our envisioned ministry was also a subtle play on our pastor's dreaded nickname, "Barney." Since our idea was to duplicate effective pastoral ministry through lay people, it seemed appropriate to link our effort to the quality care we had always received from our senior pastor and his wife, Montelle.

Barnabas Ministry it was, then.

As we were busy organizing the Barnabas Ministry, Pastor Hardwick actually preached a sermon about Barnabas. He had no idea what we were doing because we had not presented the idea yet. We got a good laugh out of that.

*Our church was doing what we had hoped: becoming a womb for new ministries and businesses.*

Like most all things, the Barnabas Ministry was, at least at first, more talk than reality. It was just a fancy name for our intention to touch the congregation and city through volunteers instead of through a massive staff. However, Donnie and Cris soon had enlisted dozens of people and organized them under the direction of good leaders.

Barnabas had a funeral and grief department, a counseling and recovery department, a hospital visitation department, a financial counseling department. It even had a department to care for our widows and single moms. In time, several of these departments became major ministries in their own right, such as Financial Peace and Life Care. Our church was doing what we had hoped: becoming a womb for new ministries and businesses.

## Life Care and Recovery Groups

Life Care was an outgrowth of our recovery department, which had originally been the dream of Lynn Husband. However, Lynn quickly discovered that her full time counseling load left her little time to run a church program. So she trained several group leaders to carry on the work of basic care. She also introduced recovery ideas to our congregation.

Viewing church life from the perspective of family systems was suspect at the time. Most church leaders still seemed to have little knowledge of the high degree of dysfunction that existed within their churches (or for that matter, within themselves.) However, using the insights of the recovery movement to help churches was actually like carrying "coals to Newcastle." Alcoholics Anonymous and the recovery movement it birthed was a child of the Christian church. The church had sheltered its early formative years and provided its basic beliefs. Unlike the clinical psychology of that era, with its emphasis upon rooting out hidden motivators for dysfunctional behavior with a psychiatrist, the recovery movement grew from the Christian belief that people are healed when they "confess their faults one to another." Christians believe that when two or three are gathered in the Lord's Name, the Holy Spirit works to deliver those who are bound. However, God wishes to be invited into a person's life through a spiritual act called repentance.

The recovery movement secularized the terms of this process of healing to help non-Christians (and those who had been harmed by churches). However, the structures of recovery were deeply grounded in biblical teaching about spiritual growth. As Lynn repeatedly taught us, it was our job to carry recovery back to the church because the church had

90

largely neglected the work of repentance, confession, absolution and transformation of the self.

She finally persuaded several of us to form a Twelve Step group for the summer "to learn how it works."

Well, heck! We did find out how it works!

Unfortunately, we also discovered that recovery often involves pain. For me, at least, that pain became the motivation for delaying my own recovery journey several years. Most of our church leaders, like our counterparts in other churches, were just not ready yet to acknowledge how deeply affected church staffs and structures were by the dislocation, alienation and personal identity crisis affecting the culture at large.

Despite the powerful work our church was doing at the time, we desperately needed someone to shine the light on all the sexual, emotional and organizational dysfunction around us. Time would reveal all of that of course, but in the meantime we at least had the good sense to allow recovery groups in our church "to help all those poor people who needed it."

In 1992, John Dyson, our youth pastor, asked Kenny Mauck to help the church develop the Barnabas Ministry further and specifically to organize our recsovery ministry. Within a short two years, the explosion of groups and group leaders that were the fruit of his work required full time staff oversight. So the church hired Kenny to do that.

The recovery ministry soon became so successful that it was occupying huge portions of the campus throughout the week. Kenny was now responsible for the entire Barnabas Ministry and needed to grow a leadership structure to stabilize it. He asked Lynn Husband and Dave Ramsey to join him in leading all aspects of our pastoral care system. By then, the overwhelming amount of our church's pastoral care

91

was provided by trained lay led volunteers. It had become the well oiled machine Donnie Wood had envisioned and Kenny had developed. It functioned without much of a budget and with very few paid staff. Until the late nineties, when some major tragedies shook our church, Barnabas provided much of the personal touch that holds a community together.

For a number of reasons, soon after the beginning of the new century, the church decided to discontinue its counseling ministry. Kenny, at first distraught, decided to begin a for-profit counseling center in his home. From that modest beginning would come LifeCare, the nation's largest faith-based mental health system. Since that time, LifeCare has continued to expand, spinning off many types of for-profit and not-for-profit care systems.

It currently operates with 200 employees in forty-five Tennessee counties. It is the fruit, not only of excellent mental health workers, but of a unique approach to building organizations that harness the energies of creative individuals.

Having already known this portion of Kenny's story, I was delighted when he recently shared another piece of his journey.

*"Upon hearing your sermon, "Let the River Run," I was so inspired! Something leapt within me, and I hid it deep within my soul. I had a vision, but was afraid that people wouldn't believe me if I shared it. Soon after, I met a young child who challenged me to take that hidden message and make the first step that had been birthed in me through Jesus Christ. This child, and what he did, would change my life forever.*

*In 1992, I worked as a counselor for a summer school program that helped mentally and emotionally disturbed children. One boy, whom I will call 'Carlos' for confidentiality* reasons, stood out to me from the start. He was one of the most anxious children I had ever met. We couldn't find his history chart, and the only things that we knew were that he was a particularly humorous eight year old African American boy who liked to take flying leaps into the trash can for the other kids' amusement. Every day, Carlos would ask me when the snack was coming. It really got under my skin that this kid continued to ask me about the snack. Every day I told him the same thing, that to not worry, his snack was coming. After many weeks of trash cans and snacks, I finally located the therapist who had Carlos' family history chart.

I discovered that Carlos was the son of a prostitute. When he was four, he and his baby brother were often left alone in their apartment while their cocaine addicted mother spent food money on her addictions and night life. The neighbors often were annoyed by the loud crying from the apartment. However, it wasn't until the neighbors heard crying for days on end that the police were called. The police record stated that two children were found. The older brother was crying in frustration because he was attempting to feed his baby brother spoiled milk, and the baby wouldn't take it.

The next day at recess, as I watched Carlos play, I wept. This little child had awoken the passion of the sermon that I had hid in my heart. I walked over to Carlos, picked him up and whispered fiercely, "I will never forget you! It might take an army, but I am ready. God will provide the people, the money, and will work with my shortcomings."

Now nearly 18 years later, with hundreds of employees throughout Middle Tennessee area, I can truly say, I have let the let the river run! I still know Carlos, and I check in on him from time to time. I have only shared his name with two attorneys and my wife all these years. I am proud to say he is *still living with the two foster parents God gave him, and he found the care and love that God had in store for him.*

*This is the reason for my being here on this earth, to love the unloved, to care for those with no hope; this is who I was called to be! God has called my wife and me to love the endangered saints in our congregations, the orphans and widows. A little boy and a sermon changed my life forever. God gave me the vision, and then gave me through others the ability to unlock that vision and see it to fruition."*

## What Is Church Administration?

Modern churches of any size have managers, administrators or executive pastors. In fact, churches of any size anywhere have some sort of management system, formal or informal. Once a church has significant numbers of people, acquires property, pays salaries to employees, or creates systems to comply with by-law requirements, some person or a group of persons emerge who specialize in systems creation and management.

In the last many years, churches have increasingly incorporated organizational models developed within the secular business community. For the most part, this has produced a more efficient corporate church life. However, there has been a downside to this shift in church work. When it comes to church as a corporation, it is tempting to gradually recreate church life in the image of business structure instead of using insights gleaned from business to improve the services of the church. When that occurs, spiritual life can become a romantic value more praised on Sunday than observed Monday through Friday.

Church administration is not, and cannot be allowed to become, imported systems of values and methods from secular corporate life. Like other Christianized systems of secular thought - Christian psychology comes to mind - trying to build a spiritual structure upon a secular foundation always morphs the entity it serves into a secular corporation.

The word "secular" comes from Latin. It simply means, "the world." As a people who are "in the world but not of the world," we are called to observe, learn from and serve the world. We must not shift our loyalties to the world. Christian values, aims and means sometimes differ sharply from those of secular enterprise, even wholesome and productive ones. Therefore, church administration must develop from biblical principles. We can learn from secular examples and theories but we must run God's house in God's ways which we learn from God's word.

* * *

*However, measurement tools we use to manage personnel and budget are hardly value-neutral.*

* * *

This implies that church administrators must work out of their spiritual gifts and biblical training, even as they apply what they learn from secular sources. In the end, money is money. People are people. Both money and people function similarly in a bank or a church. However, measurement tools we use to manage personnel and budget are hardly value-neutral. Such tools are prepared in the light of someone's priorities and someone's view of life. We must evaluate that source and its assumptions before adopting the management tools and techniques it offers.

This came home to me once while listening to Pastor Hardwick teach on the parable of the sower. He remarked how the vine planted by the Heavenly Father can become something other than what He intended. Churches can mutate. When he said that, I had a chill. I began to meditate on how churches can gradually turn from the gospel. I became

95

especially alarmed at what might be happening in American church life because we were so aggressively restructuring spiritual life around business models.

A few weeks later, I happened to read a chapter from The Practical Cogitator by Walter H. Hamilton.

Hamilton was an American physician. He wrote the essay I was reading at the end of a long and distinguished career. During his lifetime (1881-1958), he had watched his chosen profession go through tremendous changes. He says that when he began his career, the American family doctor believed he was following a sacred calling - to heal the sick. As he ended his career, Hamilton said, the American physician had become a person who makes a living by means of healing the sick. This difference, he felt, had resulted in a shift in the discipline we used to call the "healing arts," but which is now thought of as the "medical industry."

All institutions and professions organize themselves around a few central values. Hamilton felt that in our country, what usually becomes the core values of any organization are those of the business culture.

If he is right - and can he be wrong? – what he has observed can help us make sense about how things really work, as opposed to how we wish things worked.

Business is not only a means of economic production. It is a way of life, a philosophy, and a hierarchy of values. A secular business culture usually embraces values like these:

1. Find the bottom line as quickly as possible (do what "works").
2. Produce what the public will purchase.
3. Organize around financial profitability.

These three business principles make for strong corporations. In a for-profit corporation, they are essential. The question is what happens if a very different kind of institution, one historically organized around other central values, adopts these values and makes them the core of that enterprise?

Dr. Hamilton was concerned about what happens to medicine as it becomes a for-profit enterprise. We can also speculate about academic or political entities. What happens to art if it adopts a for-profit corporate culture?

More importantly, what happens to a church?

Even the most fervent proponents of free enterprise get weary if they are always placed in the role of a "consumer." We have all felt like C. S. Lewis, who wrote on one occasion: "I wish we didn't live in a world where buying and selling things (especially selling) seems to have become almost more important than either producing or using them."[1]

We are all consumers, of course. However, being little more than a consumer is demeaning. We want to be more than a consumer to someone, at least in some area of life. We also become tired of being merchants, constantly urging someone to accept some deal, always in a rush to "do something productive." If all we do is buy and sell, we become dehumanized. Sometime, somewhere, with someone, we just want to be.

The fact is, neither consumers nor marketers are the source of a culture's meaning. The source of a culture's meaning is its artists; and by "artists" I mean those who create things that were not there before.

We don't study Alexander Hamilton's budget; we study the Bill of Rights. We don't memorize Secretary of State Seward's foreign policy; we memorize Lincoln's Gettysburg

97

Address. We determine our personal meaning, and that of our institutions, by the vision that tells us why they exist. Only when we know that an institution exists to accomplish something we believe in, do we really care about keeping it solvent.

*• • •*
*The spiritual quest involves conversation, prayer, reflection and even leisure.*
*• • •*

In other words, business values are indispensable for all institutions. However, they are central only in those entities organized for making profit. When those same values become central in not-for-profit-organization, they tend to recreate those organizations into entities like those for which the values were created.

Not-for-profit organizations must remain solvent. To expand, they must raise and manage capital. Those things require someone in that organization with business skills. However, those skills must be applied in a different manner than in a for-profit institution. Otherwise, the original purpose of the institution will erode.

For example, artists and visionaries often have a difficult time proving their short term "worth" in a financially driven institution. Therefore, a for-profit culture often eliminates the mystic, the philosopher, the artist, and others with dispositions and giftings deemed impractical in such institutions. For a church of course, eliminating such people results in its spiritual death. After all, those were the sort of people Christ and his apostles were.

Thus, even if the machinery of an overly institutionalized church continues to function, even if its assets keep growing, its life will slowly drain away. A believer, who doesn't live by bread alone, seeks something in his church other than efficiency or even solvency.

The spiritual quest involves conversation, prayer, reflection and even leisure. So a church must always make room for such things, though they are not often regarded as "profitable" activities in a "for-profit" institution. For the church, the proclamation of the gospel and the care of hurting humanity defines and empowers everything. Those sorts of things must be kept central to its work. Otherwise, it mutates into a parody of church life.

Since it is chiefly a church administrator's responsibility to organize and manage a church in ways consistent with the church's unique mission, it is essential that we view church administration as a spiritual gift; not merely as a pragmatic necessity.

So what should we call that part of church leadership that looks after the material assets of the congregation; that structures church activities to become effective and wholesome? How is this part of church work supposed to function, if not like a secular business?

Biblically speaking, church administration is stewardship.

A church administrator is thus a person with gifts for organizing people, strategically managing finances, and creating the kinds of policies that empower the church's vision. A church administrator must therefore be a believer, know what the scriptures teach about stewardship, understand the values of the Kingdom of God, and lastly, understand and authentically affirm, the vision of the local church which he or she serves.

A church administrator is a spiritual leader, an elder of the church if you will. Therefore, he or she must possess the level of spiritual maturity that can sustain the attacks of the Evil One upon all spiritual leaders.

Like worship leaders and preachers, administrators face spiritual dangers unique to their calling. Perhaps the most serious of these dangers is the temptation to shift the church's financial and organizational priorities away from the support of the church's spiritual life and toward the support and expansion of its institutional life.

⚡ This is why a church must be pastorally led rather than administratively controlled.

There is an excellent example of that principle in political life.

The founding fathers of the United States made a long-reaching decision when they placed our military under civilian control. Although we have had presidents who were once military officers, they all governed as civilians. In the same way, church life must be led by pastors, who are usually not administratively gifted. A wise pastor will certainly lean heavily upon gifted and trained administrators but will also fiercely guard the church's vision, values, and ethics. He will not allow pragmatic corporate culture to gradually ignore the sovereignly unpredictable Holy Spirit, the Giver of Life, who lives at the core of the church.

Just as spiritual leaders must not allow a church's worship to degenerate into mere entertainment, so they must resist the tendency of efficient church administration to degenerate into institutional control.

In the season of our greatest spiritual impact, Christ Church administrators and organizers facilitated the gifts of our people. They discerned what God was doing and tried to structure around the congregation's natural life with as little control as necessary to maintain biblical order, legal compliance and ethical performance. Our administrators acted like traffic cops; keeping us from running into one another as we went our various ways. They didn't try to take

100

away our steering wheels. They just helped us get from place to place in the most effective and safe way.

### David Cavender and Spiritual Gifts Assessment

There's no way we could end this chapter without a word about David Cavender. He came to Christ Church from the K-Mart Corporation, where he had worked as a regional manager. As our first full time church administrator, he had his work cut out for him.

We are a creative and unruly group! Many of us are ministers, and they usually mix with administrators like oil and water. So he had days of wanting to just pull out his hair.

In a short time though, Dave began to organize the church around spiritual gifts, like people such as Dan Miller and Edsel Charles were already encouraging us to do. That implied that we had to discover our gifts.

Although it is common now for churches to take new members through a spiritual gifts assessment, it was unusual in those days. Dave not only taught this church to do it and then organize church life around it, he began travelling to teach other churches to do it.

Since then, church administration has become widely recognized as a legitimate spiritual calling. It is now well-respected and understood in church life. Dave was one of the first waves of this vital part of God's Church. He and his generation of administrators discovered how to apply the calling of steward to our times and our circumstances and deserves our respect.

They create the banks for our river – not to control it but to define and focus its flow. Without such people, visionary leaders will inspire people to do ill-defined and poorly planned things. That nearly always leads to frustration and disillusionment.

101

Dave Cavender, Donnie Wood and all our other managers, organizers, accountants and planners helped this river flow, effectively, into the future.

# DANCING WITH THE RIVER

*How God Anointed Our Art*

Landy Gardner moved to Nashville in 1976 to begin a design business. He came to Christ Church because his father, a well known Pentecostal leader, had spoken here many times. He had hardly settled before Pastor Hardwick asked him to begin a choir.

Landy had helped lead choirs since his teens. His parents were musical and the churches they pastored in South Bend, Indiana and Huntington, West Virginia, had been known for their high energy music. However, Landy had not come to Nashville to start a choir. For one thing, Christ Church was at that time, a very modest size congregation in Woodbine. A choir would be larger than the congregation! For another reason, Landy wanted to start a business.

Pastor Hardwick was insistent however, and soon Landy had a group of twenty people meeting to practice. They had to practice in the Woodlawn Cemetery chapel though, because the church was sharing its facilities with another congregation.

Construction was underway at the property on Old Hickory Boulevard where the church would soon explode in growth.

When the new church was complete in 1977, Pastor Hardwick asked Landy to prepare the choir for a concert. He had a piano player by that time but had to hire the rest of the band. The concert was a tremendous hit however and soon the church began to attract skilled musicians who were delighted to play for what was quickly becoming a world class gospel choir.

Some traumatic events in Landy's personal and business life nearly aborted the success of the Christ Church choir. Without an income or any apparent hope of one, he thought seriously of accepting an offer to become the administrator of Christ Temple in Huntington, West Virginia. However, two events changed his mind: a Christ Church member offered to pay $300.00 a month for him to keep leading the choir, and, he landed his first major design job. For several months after that, he lived with the Hardwick family and worked to recover his life in Nashville.

It was a good thing he decided to stay! In 1976, Joy Dyson came for a choir concert. She had already established herself as a major gospel performer. Having sung all her life in churches and conferences, she had been named Female Vocalist of the Year in 1976. Now, also going through a personal crisis, she was adrift and looking for a new place of service. Although she thought she was finished with music, music was not finished with her.

Landy called her one evening in desperation because all of his vocalists were sick and he had scheduled a choir concert in Dickson, Tennessee. He asked Joy if she would fill in for his absent soloist. She could learn the songs on the way to the concert, he said!

A friendship between Landy and Joy became a romance and then, in 1980, a marriage.

Joy's contribution helped take the choir to an entirely new level. She had been trained in the same musical tradition as Landy and knew how to teach parts by rote. This is what had distinguished African-American choirs from the more European rooted musical tradition.

European choral music requires at least a modest level of formal musical training because choir members read the notes to be sung from a written score. In contrast, the Black Gospel tradition focuses on communicating passion by discovering the natural harmonies suggested by the informed and experienced intuition of a choir leader. This was Landy and Joy's method. It allowed them to develop a sound that was unique at the time, at least for our largely Caucasian choir.

In the Black Gospel tradition, choir directors like James Cleveland had been holding enormous music clinics for years. However, White audiences were just beginning to discover these Black artists, and others, such as Edwin and Walter Hawkins, and Andrae Crouch. However, few White churches were crossing yet over into the genre. The sounds and energy produced by Black choirs seemed mysterious and impossible to duplicate to most White choir directors. It was not mysterious at all for Landy and Joy; they had been raised on that music.

Our band members followed that same musical path. Phil Kristianson, a highly trained classical pianist, had also worked with Andrae Crouch and other Church of God in Christ musical groups. He brought a powerful blend of Black Gospel and classical structure to the instrumental sound of Christ Church.

The result of these musical innovations was something like what Phil Jackson describes in his book, *Sacred Hoops*.

Raised Pentecostal, Jackson had become a Zen Buddhist by the time he was coach of the Chicago Bulls and the Los Angeles Lakers. In his book, Jackson describes how his religious journey had impacted his famous coaching style, which might by summed up in the motto, "when you work, work; when you play, play." While other coaches ran around yelling at their players, Jackson often appeared to be doing nothing at all. However, he actually worked hard with his players, practicing maneuver after maneuver. The game was not for that, Jackson thought. It was for playing. He wanted his players to play, joyfully and creatively.

Jackson talks about how once a team has practiced much and the members have come to know one another well, a certain kind of flow can emerge at game time in which the players invent maneuvers on the spot. Often their intuition proves to be the right way to go. At that point, too much direction from the coach can ruin the flow, turning the game into a boring regurgitation of highly structured game plans.

*That was not because the choir created our church culture exactly, but because it expressed it so well.*

Landy and Joy's method of choral arrangement and practice, now joined with the musical genius of the likes of Phil and other professional studio musicians, raised the bar for the entire genre of gospel choir music. Like Jackson would do with sports, the Gardners would do with music, focus on developing a musical team that knew how to "go with the flow."

It is important to understand the role of the Christ Church choir in the life of our church. We were used to the jokes around town about being a "congregation organized around a choir." Most of us didn't even find it offensive. We all knew that our choir represented the essence of Christ Church. That was not because the choir created our church culture exactly, but because it expressed it so well.

106

The Christ Church worship experience flowed from the choir and indirectly, from Landy and Joy. I say that not because they dominated our worship experience in any way but because they taught our choir to model artistic and spiritual freedom within limits. Even though our worship service was carefully planned, the pastors, worship leaders, band and congregation came to know that things never went exactly to plan. The various players flowed in and out of the plan as the Spirit moved.

An unplanned guitar solo might breakout one Sunday in the middle of a praise chorus, or someone might start a song that had not been planned at all. To the congregation it felt like things were being put together on the spot - which wasn't really the case. However, the spontaneity was genuine, nonetheless because of the innovation that continually occurred. It was like jazz, where musicians spontaneously innovate around a known and rehearsed theme. Our genre was not jazz but the process was very much like that.

How could it have been otherwise with the likes of a Lindell Cooley, our worship leader? Although he would later become known as the worship pastor during the Brownsville revival, Lindell was, for us, a fresh young piano player from Alabama who led us in worship each week. He was a force of nature: spontaneously combustible but at the same time the most gentle and kind person imaginable.

He was as much fun as any human being I have ever met. He once wrote a set of worship songs for Charismatics, based on scripture passages that were never meant to be sung. He would sing them for us until we were laughing so hard we made him stop. Underneath all that fun however, was a heart after God that lifted our spirits and took us into times of profound worship.

Lindell was representative of many of our musicians at the time. Each contributed something special to the worship culture Landy and Joy had created and which became so important in the transformation of so many lives.

Our choir's music gained increasing notoriety and influence during that time. As a result, we had to hold our concerts in the Grand Ole Opry house for several years with some of Nashville's best known musical celebrities.

Ron Griffin, who was with StarSong Music Company at the time, produced a well received project called Hand in Hand. The printed material from that project helped hundreds of church choirs around the country reproduce the worship experience we had begun to take for granted. Three more successful projects were released on Prism. By the mid-nineties, the Christ Church Choir was enjoying a very wide circle of notoriety within English-speaking Evangelical churches.

It is important to note that while the choir had a number of powerful voices and performers, its success required the hard work of dozens of people. Most of them were volunteers, although some became part-time employees as the years passed. Stephen and Miriam Tedeschi, Beth Kolwyck and others brought the organization and performance to increasingly high levels, for example. However, the effectiveness of the whole was always greater than its individual parts. The choir was anointed; that is what made its performance so dynamic.

## Global Connections

As we mentioned in the chapter on missions, Christ Church had not been a missions focused assembly before the late eighties. The people of the congregation had been generous with their money when asked to contribute toward missions projects but Middle Tennessee was a regional city well into the nineteen eighties. The globalization of Middle Tennessee culture came as a shock to those who grew up here, and to some extent, is still a shock today.

At any rate, the choir was the first part of our church to make any serious international connections. In 1984, the Israeli government had invited the choir to sing in Bethlehem on Christmas Eve. They were supposed to sing in the very first minutes of Christmas Day. The choir accepted the invitation and flew to Israel.

*The globalization of Middle Tennessee culture came as a shock to those who grew up here, and to some extent, is still a shock today.*

As the hours of Christmas Eve went by however, the crowd in the square was not in a sacred mood. The atmosphere turned dangerous and rowdy. The mood turned when Marlys Kroon began to sing, "O Little Town of Bethlehem." The audience quickly became respectful and attentive after that.

This would be merely the first of many international choir events. Our musicians had tasted global culture and would not be able to resist the growing calls of international adventure.

By 1993, our new-found missions vision was in full bloom. The many Russian connections that we had made and that others had made for us were quickly changing the face of our congregation. So when the choir was invited to travel to the Ukraine, it no longer seemed strange. The question was simply about how to raise the funds.

The Missions Department (under the leadership of Gerhardt Richter) had an intense debate that year about spending the huge sum required to send our choir to the

Ukraine. Many on the Missions committee were reluctant to use our limited missions budget on ourselves. Others believed that because music was the heart of our congregation, we would reap many long-range benefits from making a strategic investment to expose our music leaders to the world. The Missions Department finally accepted this strategy and set aside the lion's share of the missions budget that year to send the choir on their historic trip.

So the choir learned songs in Russian and Ukrainian and set out on a tour of the Ukraine. The Ukrainian people responded warmly, both to the music and to the gospel. As for our choir members, they became keenly aware of the spiritual need of the world's peoples and of our local church's responsibility to help meet that need.

Our strategy had proved effective. Many choir members returned from the Ukraine profoundly moved. They became some of our most enthusiastic mission supporters and remain so to this day.

### Anointed Arts

Although the choir was the core of our artistic expression, it was not the only expression of the arts in Christ Church. Numerous entertainers, producers and writers came to the church or from the church. Some only visited from time to time. Others actually joined the church. There was something about the artistic climate that seemed to lift artistic expression to new levels. As our artists grew their spiritual lives together, they gathered material that they molded into unique expressions of artistry and spirituality.

Many years later, Regi Stone would write his song, *Here in This House There Is a Blessing,* because of the encouragement that he believed our community provided for artists. That blessing seemed to draw writers and performers from all around, Christian and non-Christian alike.

Our children had no idea about the fame of the artists who came to our church. To them, the artists were just friends of their parents.

I remember the morning my daughter came running through the house, amazed to have found Naomi and Wynonna Judd on TV. They had just had dinner with them the night before! They just couldn't believe they knew someone on TV.

Johnny Cash brought Waylon Jennings with him one Sunday morning. They stayed around after service to visit for a while. In my sermon that morning I had told the musicians in attendance that they needed to stop smoking pot. If they didn't, I said, they were all going to turn into cumquats.

"Pastor," Waylon said, "if smoking pot could turn a man into cumquats, my friend Willie Nelson would have become one by now!"

(I don't claim that all our musicians were instantly transformed in Christ. I'm only claiming that they attended!)

In such a creative place, surrounded by so much talent, many of us tried our hand at writing and performing.

Some of us did much more.

Patricia Cross was already a skilled and trained dancer when she came to Christ Church.

She had trained in Minneapolis under Lorand and Anna Adrianova Andahazy, of Ballet Russe. After moving to Plattsburgh, New York, she had continued her studies in Montréal as she founded her own regional ballet company, Adirondack Ballet, sponsored by the State University of New York at Plattsburgh.

In the Methodist church where she attended while living in Plattsburgh, she joined a Charismatic prayer group where she had a dramatic experience with the Holy Spirit. As a result, she experimented expressing worship through dance, by choreographing creative movement to Bach's concerto in B minor, for example. However, the ego-driven atmosphere of the professional dance world seemed increasingly at odds with her growing understanding of faith. She concluded that dance had become an idol to her and that she would leave it in pursuit of God.

*I decided that the way I could give out would be to offer my gifts of dance, not as a performer but as a teacher, to the children of the church.*

"God took me into a season of profound repentance," Patricia says. "It was like what Sheldon Vanauken describes in his book, *A Severe Mercy*, where all must be surrendered in finding the pearl of great price.

After moving to Nashville and finding Christ Church, in 1991 I stumbled into Pat Gruits class, Understanding God. As I listened each week, I gradually understood what had occurred to me in Plattsburgh. I began to become a real disciple.

The church was going through a series at the time called Blessed to Be a Blessing. On one particular Sunday, Dan preached about how we should be getting filled up at church in order to give out to the world. I decided that the way I could give out would be to offer my gifts of dance, not as a performer but as a teacher, to the children of the church.

We soon had forty-five children and we were asked to participate in the Christmas program to the piece from Messiah, *Unto Us a Child Is Born*. I put a few teenage girls in the front and dressed all the little girls up in angel costumes. Of course, none of them had much training. However, the

112

church responded so warmly and the children were so delighted that it helped open the doors for further ministry. I must say though, that there was a particularly strong anointing on the performance that night.

It was so different than the secular studios I had served in Nashville. Sometimes I was grieved by the way they dressed children and taught them such sensual moves. I'm not a prude or anything and I am not upset when the beauty of human movement is put on display. It's just that dance evokes all sorts of reactions from an audience and we have some responsibility to not evoke the wrong kind of reaction, especially when children are involved. Watching Christian children perform in all their innocence and delight was really wonderful.

Dance is really a form of "living sculpture." Like all kinds of sculpture, it communicates something. Dance tells a story. Théophile Gautier's Giselle, for example, is stunningly beautiful because it communicates such tender emotion about life and love. Making that clear to an audience requires movements of great precision. That in turn, requires enormous control over a disciplined body. Dancers who develop such a body are understandably proud of the result. However, a dancer can easily cross a line into a worship of the body. When this occurs, it is a spiritual problem for the believer.

I don't mean to say I object to "secular" dance. I think Christian artists make a mistake when they limit their gifts to communicating an overtly Christian message for Christian audiences. Some artists are probably called to do so; I think many are not. Also, "Christian" is often used as a cover up for lack of training and preparation. Sometimes I see "dancers" in churches with a "dance ministry," and it's difficult to appreciate. I acknowledge their sincerity but when you have been trained, undisciplined movement is hard to take.

I taught dance in Christ Church for ten years. When things at the church shifted, I began to feel a stirring to begin a ministry for at-risk children. I didn't know how I was going to pay for it – or for my own livelihood for that matter – but I launched out anyway.

Rejoice Ministries was the result. It took a while to get off the ground and sometimes I think it has not made it very far from the ground!

My idea was simple enough: I would offer classical and contemporary dance in an economically disadvantaged location. I would teach young children and form a relationship with them that would hopefully continue through puberty and on into young adulthood. I thought dance might well open up our students to other kinds of education and cultural experience.

We have had a lot of students go through the program now and have experienced many successes. They have performed with the Nashville Ballet, especially when they need children's parts, such as in the Nutcracker. They have performed at the  Schermerhorn and of course here at Christ Church from time to time.

People always cry when they see our kids perform. I think that is because they really do try to worship as they dance. Our students are not the most polished in the world. Some of them are pretty good, others not so much. However they are a community and God is with them."

Patricia Cross is one of the great unsung heroes of Christ Church. Like many others whom God raised up during our season of grace, she has just kept on doing what she was called to do, wondering year after year if enough money would come in to do it one more year. This polished and cultured

114

woman made a serious commitment to live simply in a difficult area of our city, reaching people many had forgotten: orphans, foster children, kids who try to sleep to the sounds of gunfire, people who it would be easy to write off, as though already lost. She has refused to do that, week after week, month after month, and year after year. In those seasons when even her church family forgot what she was doing, she just kept on working, without bitterness, relying on the Lord for provision and guidance; taking the spirit of David into the highways and the byways.

Patricia Cross is a real artist, who like her Lord, "sees things that are not as though they were."

# KEEPERS OF THE SPRING

*Christ Church Intercessors*

Anyone who attended Christ Church in years past will agree that Montelle Hardwick was the heart of our church. She was an exceptional person in every way. Mischievous, funny, loving and authentically spiritual; she created much of the culture that made our church so special.

Montelle was the senior pastor's wife. However, she never expected nor accepted any sort of special privilege. She was a sister in Christ who loved her husband, her children, and the people of God. She seemed to constantly be plotting about how to weave the people together. Especially as our membership began to broaden to include such a wide spectrum of backgrounds, Montelle worried about unity and community within the congregation.

We don't have the time or space here to tell about her many pranks and practical jokes. She didn't mind going to extreme lengths to make her stories believable as the unwitting victim got pulled into her prank. Yet, she could instantly move into prayer and worship.

I think that is what amazed me about Monetelle; she was a spiritual woman that loved to joke and laugh. Her heart was seeking God, but her feet remained firmly planted on the ground.

Her father was a saint, no doubt about it. His name, Nobel, tells you everything about him you need to know for he was as humble and godly a man as ever I met. The day he died, I went to his home and went through the cardboard box that he kept beside his recliner. It was full of names written on small slips of paper, and several pictures of missing children that he had cut out from the back of milk cartons. His wife told me that he would sit in that chair and read the names to God and plead for the Lord's intervention on behalf of those children.

His spirituality however, was entirely unassuming. I once told him that I hoped to become a holy man one day as I thought he was. He replied that he was not really holy, just old!

The story of Christ Church would not make a lot of sense apart from a number of individuals like Montelle and her father who established our spiritual culture. Others taught, organized and performed and their ministries were the ones people noticed. The intercessors and devotional leaders were much more subtle. Nonetheless, none of the better known people I will mention in this book will disagree when I say that the quality of our community was due in very large part to the group I will call the "keepers of the spring."

That description is not original. I first heard it in 1967, when my father preached a sermon I would never forget. In fact, I preached it too one Father's Day a few years ago. Dad told me afterward that he heard the story behind his sermon from Peter Marshall, chaplain of the United States Senate in the early sixties.

The setting was a little a village, in one of the world's most scenic places, the Swiss Alps. Everyone in the town seemed happy and healthy. However, the village had no money for repairs and improvements because it was passing

117

through an economically difficult time. So the town council held a meeting to discuss how to cut their expenses and make money.

One of the councilmen had been reviewing a list of town employees. He had seen something that bothered him which he brought to the attention of the council. It seems that the town had been paying a small sum each year to an employee that was simply listed in the rolls as "the keeper of the spring".

"Who is this keeper of the spring?" he demanded.

No one knew, as it turned out.

In the following days, the council members discovered that the "keeper of the spring" was an old man who lived up in the mountains above the village. Many years before, the parents and grandparents of the present council had decided to pay him this small stipend. In return, he was to keep the debris out of a little stream that ran from the glaciers down the valley to the town.

The council decided that the payment to the man, who was now very old, had really been just an act of benevolence that the town could no longer afford. Evidently, their counterparts a generation before had decided to help a nice man. Like a lot of things, the money had just been overlooked. As a result, the man had continued to receive the money year after year. At any rate, it was something the town could no longer afford. They decided to cut out from the budget the stipend for the "keeper of the spring."

They told a little boy who had been running up the mountain each month to give the old man his money, to inform him of the change. When he got the news, the old man decided to move down into the village with his niece. The council had cut out superfluous spending. The old man was happy with his niece. Everything went well for two or three years.

It was in third year that the people started getting sick. Dysentery broke out. A few old people didn't survive it. Babies started getting sick with this and that. Little by little, the happy little town got filled with sorrow, sickness and misery. No one seemed to realize what had happened.

Finally, one wise man that everyone respected made the connection between the polluted water supply and the increasing sickness. So he went to the council and asked them to reinstate the "keeper of the spring". They agreed. Soon the old man went back to work, cleaning out branches and debris from the stream high up in the hills. For a while, no one noticed much of a difference. However, by the third year the water was clean again and health began to return to the people of the village.

*In any healthy community, you can be sure that there are many people dedicated to keeping junk out of the spring.*

In any healthy community, you can be sure that there are many people dedicated to keeping junk out of the spring. That was certainly true of our community.

Sister Pearl Reed was one of them. She had been in the church almost since its beginning. She had experienced some of the greatest challenges in life a person can face but she remained dedicated to prayer, to service, and to doing whatever menial thing the church needed done. Her spiritual life was always understated and hidden away in that intimate relationship she had with God. The fruit of her life, however, was evident to all.

God sent new people to clean the spring during this season of grace though. One Sunday in 1987, as the people were coming forward for prayer, Pastor Hardwick and I looked at one another with bewilderment. We had just seen the same thing at the same time. A giant African-American man in a clerical collar was standing with arms raised with everyone else. His face glowed. There was no doubt that he was someone special, we just didn't know who.

We soon discovered that he was Bishop Ralph Houston, who had pastored many years in Watts in L.A., and had just relocated to Nashville. He had been recently consecrated bishop in his denomination, and had moved from California to the dioceses he had been appointed to serve. He had decided that he should not settle his family in one of the churches he was overseeing but to a neutral location.

The Bishop became an enormous blessing to all of us. It would be a long time before we realized what all he had done for God's kingdom and how much wisdom he really had to offer. To give you some idea of his accomplishments, Mayor Bradley had once asked him to head the delegation to welcome Pope John Paul when the pope visited Los Angeles.

("I went because the mayor asked me," Bishop Houston said. "I just didn't know what I thought about meeting the pope. Then, when he walked down the steps of the plane, I just put out my hand and said, Brother John Paul, welcome to Los Angeles. And that little White brother ignored my hand, hugged me and said, 'Brother, thank you. I am happy to be in Los Angeles. I looked into his eyes and saw just another Christian who loved the Lord.")

Houston was a busy man, but when he was in town he visited hospitals, preached, prayed, and did whatever we asked him to do. He was especially interested in the spiritual growth of our young leaders, and kept his home open to meet with them.

The Houstons became like grandparents to our congregation and helped ease the way as we became an increasingly diverse church.

## The Three Js

There is a portrait in the entrance of the Christ Church prayer chapel. Most people now have no idea who the man is who smiles at them as they enter that space to pray. He wouldn't mind. He might even laugh to think we would hang his portrait anywhere in the church. His name was Jim; and he was a servant of the Lord.

When Jim Enoch went to Germany in World War II, he carried with him a piece of paper from his young bride. On the paper, Sally had written "I will enable you. I will shield you. I will deliver you." In every battle of the war, he read that paper and confessed those words. They became his mantra.

When the war was over, Jim turned to another war. For the rest of his life, he battled the forces of darkness that kill, steal and destroy. He was a mighty warrior whom God uniquely gifted to see into the heart of things.

In the mid seventies, the Lord called Jim and Sally to Christ Church. Jim had a strong impression that God was going to visit the little congregation and that his ministry of prayer and prophetic word would be needed. So as he sold real estate - very successfully, I should add – he ministered to our flock in intercessory prayer and spiritual direction.

He was right. In the early eighties, he asked his friend Jack Hughes to begin meeting with him once a week for prayer. After several false starts and stops, they began meeting each Monday night in the Wallace House, a private residence that we tore down in the late eighties to build our present sanctuary. After only a few weeks, they felt that God

121

was calling them to add one more member to their prayer team and that it should be John Saucier.

That's how the three Js came to be: Jim, Jack and John. We all used to say the 4 Js though, because we knew that the fourth "J" was the one that made all the difference!

Jack Hughes was our resident genius, one of the first wave of people to study molecular biology at Vanderbilt graduate school level. I once heard him say that there were not even text books for his classes because the field was so new! Genius or not, Jack was a fervent God-seeker.

John Saucier was an engineer, and in a very different field than his friend Jack. He had built a sewage and plumbing company and had worked for important building projects all over the mid-south.

God had called three unlikely friends, very different one from the other, to meet once a week. They would do that week after week, year after year, until three became two. After Jim went on to heaven, Jack and John continued praying each Monday night, and continue to do so at the time of this writing.

That's commitment!

Few Christ Church people have not had their season with the three Js in some difficult hour. Always trustworthy with private information, attentive to the needs of the people, and full of compassion for those in need, the three Js gradually became fathers in God to this congregation.

Their manner was as much a part of their ministry as their message. Jim would sometimes prophesy, often writing it down for your consideration. He never pushed, never manipulated and never sought to control others. He gave his word and left it for your consideration. Once he gave it, it was between you and God. Sometimes he said something like,

"Dan, it was either something I ate, or God is trying to tell me something about you."

He would laugh. I would laugh and he would tell me what he had to say. Sometimes it made sense, sometimes it didn't. If it didn't, I could say so and he would just leave it at that, not in the least bit offended. I must say though, I would usually discover what the word had been about sometime later. I can't recall that his words were ever really due to "something he ate."

I was in Phoenix when Jim fell asleep in the Lord. I called him and talked to him a few days before he died. At his funeral, Pastor Hardwick preached the sermon: "There was a man named Enoch who walked with God."

That can be said of all three of this special band of spiritual soldiers who have tried to watch over our souls in the most tender, compassionate, and wise way. In fact, it can be said of all the ones I have mentioned here, and ones I have not, who helped us "'oft escape the tempter's snare by thy return, sweet hour of prayer."

They have been the keepers of our spring, working tirelessly behind the scenes to keep the junk out of the river. May God remember them on the day of judgment and reward them openly for all they have done in secret.

# FINDING THE SOURCE

*How Our Teachers Connected Us to*
*Scripture and to Christian History*


I saw a stealth bomber once.

I was driving down highway 51 in Phoenix at the time, having just come through Dreamy Draw, the little stretch of mountainous desert that separates the newer, northern part of the city from the older downtown area. A large shadow suddenly fell over my car and when I looked up to see what was causing it, I nearly wrecked. I saw a gigantic bat, flying straight toward downtown Phoenix!

I was frightened. Then I remembered that the stealth was doing a fly-over the stadium for the World Series.

It's no longer a new piece of technology. However, the stealth is still impressive, and true to its name, it does rather sneak up on a place.

God also has stealth weapons. Even Christ was rather like a stealth weapon, "having no comeliness that one should desire him." Or, as Bob Dylan once put it, "who unleashed his power in an unknown hour, when no one knew." Dylan was amazed to discover that the presence and power of Christ had 'snuck up on him.' As a Jew, he was moved by the quiet way in which the Messiah had moved into history and had so completely altered it. Dylan writes that the "power" of Christ can only be seen in retrospect. Christ had not come into the world with 'guns blazing', but he "unleashed his power in an unknown hour when no one knew."

We have had a few stealth leaders in our church who worked like that. None were as mysteriously powerful as David Anderson, a printer who gradually became a highly respected teacher in our church. To call David Anderson unassuming would be a serious understatement. He spoke quietly, denied that he had anything important to offer and lurked on the edge of church life, uninterested in any office, position or power. He just led Bible studies for those who showed up. He didn't advertise. He didn't promote. He just opened up the scripture and taught.

David Anderson's greatest contribution to our church was probably his Bethel Course. He didn't even intend to teach that! He had signed up to take the course from Dorothy Smithson, who was terrified about teaching it. She had taken the course from me, and had made a commitment to teach once completing it.

I don't want to interrupt the story, but I should say something about Bethel because it was one of a handful of classes that seriously impacted our congregation.

As an example of how much it affected people: Ron Griffin was an extremely successful music producer. One night in a Bethel class, as we discussed the rich young ruler, he heard a call from God. Within the year, he had sold his business and was moving to Breckenridge, Colorado. He joined St. John's Episcopal Church, taught Sunday school, became a priest, and led that congregation into its season of greatest growth!

Bethel did that to people.

Bethel is a two year overview of the Bible. It uses iconic images - cartoons would probably be an inappropriate description - to help a student memorize basic elements of scripture each week. At the end of the course, the Bethel student should know all the books of the Bible, its most important stories, and the central themes that run through the Old and New Testaments.

Pastor Hardwick and I had a seen a presentation of the Bethel Bible Course at the Crystal Cathedral in Los Angeles. We decided we needed it in our congregation. So, we both scheduled time in Madison, Wisconsin to go through the training, along with John Dyson, our youth pastor.

*The power of David's teaching was the encounter a student had with a Bible-soaked man who just opened up his mouth and allowed the Word to pour out.*

I went through the training first and I began the first class. Pastor Hardwick and John Dyson followed with another class a semester later. I started with a dozen students or so, most of whom did not intend to teach it after completion. In fact so few of them committed to teach that Dorothy Smithson had pity on me and had signed up to teach once she was through the training. That's where David Anderson comes in. He joined her class.

Dorothy soon realized that David knew a lot about the scripture. So, she took it upon herself to ask him to help her teach. He agreed. Without even having taken the training, he taught the course. More like it was intended to be taught than any of the rest of us!

Those who heard David teach were captivated by his presentation. However, they could never describe why. The power of David's teaching was the scripture itself. It was not his style, or a display of his brilliance. The power of David's teaching was the encounter a student had with a Bible-soaked man who just opened up his mouth and allowed the Word to pour out. The presence of God accompanied his words, because he knew more than anyone that the words were not his to begin with.

David Anderson was a "stealth bomber." God used him to "unleash His power in an unknown hour when no one knew." We are still benefiting from that deposit of grace.

Now, there was nothing stealth-like about Pat Gruits. She was more like heavy artillery that an army moves in purposefully, visibly, with the enemy fully aware of what is going on. She came to Nashville with the intention of catechizing us; rooting us in the basic doctrines and practices of the Christian faith.

Her mother was the famous Ma Beall, founder of Bethesda Missionary Temple. A center for what came to be known as the 'Latter Rain revival,' Bethesda was unusually committed to the study of theology. The Beall family was extraordinarily gifted teachers and they insisted that the Charismatic experience was legitimate if and only when it respected biblical boundaries. To ensure that those boundaries remain viable and firm, they decided to restore the ancient practice of catechism.

It would be difficult for most people today to understand how controversial this was. To Pentecostals, catechism was "catholic." It was formalism, legalism, a quenching of the spirit. Why, this would undermine the very freedom that Pentecostals had recovered after long centuries of ecclesiastical oppression, people warned.

The Bealls persisted. Their people would be catechized. They would learn the creeds, the Ten Commandments, the Books of the Bible, the central doctrines of the church, and how to apply these to everyday life. Furthermore, students would actually experience the things being studied. They would be baptized, receive communion and be filled with the

Holy Spirit. The people of Bethesda would be disciples, not just church attendees.

Pastor Hardwick and Montelle loved the Bealls, especially loved Patricia Gruits, Ma Beall's daughter. They invited her to Nashville to catechize the hundreds of new people who had come to Christ Church because we too needed a firm foundation for our congregation.

Their idea was for Patricia to teach a group of leaders who would then teach everyone else. We would make her catechism mandatory for all future church leaders, thus ensuring the health of our biblical and theological foundation. The leader of the effort would be James Boutwell, a former Pentecostal presbyter of our area who had become an elder in our church. Unfortunately, Boutwell died suddenly of a heart attack. So I was asked to continue the program.

My assistant was Beverly Robbins, who, as it turned out, was a very good teacher. She became an apprentice to both Patricia Gruits and me, and soon had become a gifted catechist in her own right. As the years unfolded, Beverly actually catechized more of Christ Church's people than anyone else.

### Why is Teaching Important?

Biblical and theological teaching is the skeleton of a healthy church. Like the skeleton of any healthy mammal, a church's doctrinal structure should be nearly invisible. Most people do not find skeletons attractive. One rarely hears of a young man proposing to a woman because he finds "her skeleton irresistible." The same holds for people looking for a church. Potential members choose a church based on programs for youth, music style, or even parking accessibility. Decades of research have repeatedly proven this. However, a deceased skeleton is more dangerous most of the time than deceased skin because skin is visible. Any skin defect immediately alarms us. In the same way, a church youth program that doesn't work is going to get someone's attention quickly. A lack of biblical and theological education in the church may not alarm anyone. In the end though, spiritual life can survive bad church music; it cannot survive biblical ignorance, at least for long.

Bishop Fitzsimmons Allison's delightful little book, <u>The Cruelty of Heresy</u>, clearly makes this case. It is well worth a church leader's time to read it.

* * *

*In the end though, spiritual life can survive bad church music; it cannot survive biblical ignorance, at least for long.*

* * *

Christ Church has certainly gone through seasons in which we did not emphasize Bible teaching. Nonetheless, Christ Church has always had a culture of reading and study. Historically, that has been rare for American Pentecostal and Charismatic congregations.

In fact, there is often an undercurrent of hostility in the Pentecostal and Charismatic churches toward formal biblical and theological study.

A quick glance at many popular television speakers makes my point. With some notable exceptions, Charismatic Christianity has often encouraged a disdain toward academic life in general, and toward theological training in particular. Christ Church has been an exception to this. We have always maintained strong connections with non-Evangelicals, even those who taught that the more dramatic gifts of the Spirit ceased after the writing of the New Testament. The reason we have maintained such relationships is simple: we wanted to remain committed to biblical scholarship and to Christian orthodoxy.

129

Many of our church leaders came from a part of the Pentecostal movement that grew increasingly sectarian, closed to other forms of the faith. As time went on, we had been forbidden to form relationships with those outside our group. Once we left all that behind, we became super sensitive to the dangers of sectarian attitudes and to theological sloth.

It is often difficult to maintain a church's focus on teaching. In times of crisis,(Christ Church has had its share of those) it just doesn't come across as that important. In such times, a church can become neglectful of teaching the doctrines of the faith. Few will complain, as they most certainly will if the music isn't good. However, God has kept teachers among us who kept on teaching, even though they were not paid, sometimes had a difficult time finding a room, and were often confined to the edge of our church life. They kept teaching the Word because they had a commission from God to do so.

In the years that this book addresses, I was in my early thirties. Preaching to hundreds of people every week was a heady experience. Sometimes, after a sermon that the people seemed to really enjoy, David Anderson would wait in line to add his compliments to those of others. Then he would add this: "Brother Dan, remember that God resists the proud but gives grace to the humble."

From most people, that scripture would come across as a snide, sanctimonious comment, meant to cut down someone the speaker consider to be an arrogant young punk. David didn't mean it that way. He loved me and was delighted with my gifts. He was also aware that the Evil One would like nothing better than to destroy my soul with early success, and the praise of crowds was an especially powerful tool to do that. He was watching out for me. I knew that and loved him for it.

He watched out for my soul. Good teachers always do that; they bring to our remembrance the teachings of the scripture and mold our spiritual lives by the power of the Word.

# Three Streams Converge

In the fall of 1993, Terry Mattingly, a professor at Milligan College and a syndicated columnist, wrote a piece about Christ Church and published it in hundreds of the nation's newspapers.

I was shocked when I read the article because I had not known about it in advance. Neither did I have any idea how much that article would change my life. For one thing, it would soon mark me as a strident opponent to liberal Christianity; I didn't mind that. What would become much more painful was the reaction from many of my Pentecostal friends.

Mattingly began by describing a worship service at the Church of St. John the Divine, in New York City. He told how various gods and goddess of antiquity were invoked in the service and then continued with a warning about the approaching meltdown of mainline Christianity in America. He backed up his claim with quotes from American church leaders and gave specific examples of their various blasphemous and heretical actions.

Then he shifted gears with the following:

"Not long after the St. Francis service at St. John the Divine, I attended another unusual communion service.

In this case, I was in Nashville working on several articles about the Jerusalem of country music. On another sunny Sunday morning, I slipped into a pew at Christ (Pentecostal) Church, a booming congregation attended by many professional musicians. I was prepared for an emotionally uplifting service, a fiery sermon and powerful music.

Then it came time for the Lord's Supper.

The faithful bowed their heads as associate pastor Dan Scott raised his arms and began to pray: ``Almighty God, to you all hearts are open, all desires known, and from you no secrets are hid: Cleanse the thoughts of our hearts by the inspiration of your Holy Spirit, that we may perfectly love you, and worthily magnify your Holy Name; through Christ our Lord."

And all the people said, ``Amen."

Once again, I was caught off guard and it was fair to ask: What was going on?

In his book, The Emerging American Church, Scott has offered his answer. He is convinced that creeds, sacraments and apostolic teaching have never been more relevant to the lives of people caught in a whirlpool of change. But the powers that be and many ``high potentates" in churches are dashing off to worship at the altar of relevance, according to Scott.

But millions of Americans don't want to go.

Instead, they are joining ``churches like ours, churches led by people so backward ... that they still believe in a physical resurrection, in the Holy Scriptures, in the effectiveness of the sacraments, in the immutability of God's law, in our Savior's virgin birth and in the literal truth of his promised second return. The people excommunicated their bishops," writes Scott.

At times, it's hard to make sense of it all[3]."

At the time, I was delighted by the article. I thought it would boost book sales of The Emerging American Church, which had just been published by Bristol House. I did not expect the negative reaction from Pentecostals. I had simply not realized how our appreciation for Christian traditions at Christ Church would strike some contemporary Pentecostals as "catholic" and offensive.

The communion service Mattingly described in his article was actually the way we had been doing communion for years. In fact, it was not very different from the way I had experienced communion in my Pentecostal church in West Virginia. However, as the years had gone by, newer generations of Pentecostals had lost touch with the hymns and structure of worship that their grandparents had learned in the more traditional churches of their birth. American Pentecostalism, which grew out of Methodism after all, had originally incorporated much of that past into the new movement. One can see this very clearly even now in many African-American Pentecostal groups, (such as the Church of God in Christ, for example.) However, as the century had progressed, most White Pentecostals had gradually jettisoned their traditional roots. By the century's end, many Pentecostals looked at traditional Protestant worship with hostility.

Christ Church went another direction. Like many African-American congregations, we attempted to honor

---

[3] **http://www.tmatt.net/tmatt/freelance/wolves.htm**

traditional Protestant traditions while remaining open to contemporary moves of the Spirit. It is a balance we have maintained since the church's beginning and to which we remain committed.

## Why Christ Church Maintained
## Protestant Forms of Worship

It is difficult to tell the history of Christ Church without including some of our reasons for separating from our parent denomination. Like most such stories, this one involved pain, and still looks different from the various perspectives of those who experienced it.

It is not necessary to tell that story in detail, of course. It would not even be helpful for our purposes here. What is necessary is to explain that the denomination within which our church was birthed went through a number of political and doctrinal purges in the nineteen seventies and eighties. As a result, its original allowances for local and regional differences were replaced by an insistence on doctrinal uniformity. During that period, it also ended its historic tolerance for those members with relationships to the broader Christian world.

*Like most such stories, this one involved pain, and still looks different from the various perspectives of those who experienced it.*

Because of our deep love and respect for those Pentecostal leaders who brought us to faith (and who mentored us in ministry), our church tried for several years to maintain its formal connections with our denomination. By the early eighties however, Christ Church had become increasingly embarrassing to the denomination's newer leaders. This came to a head in 1986, when the denomination asked Pastor Hardwick to cancel a speaking engagement he had planned in a non-aligned congregation. Because the event was less than a week away, he decided to formally withdraw his membership.

It would be difficult to explain to those of younger generations how traumatic this was at the time. Nowadays, it is common for a church and its leaders to lack denominational affiliation. That is a relatively new development though. Throughout history, local churches have been expressions of larger entities. These larger bodies – denominations – have historically provided leadership, resources, and most importantly, an identity for their affiliated local churches. For these reasons, until the last few years, most pastors would have thought it rebellious and irresponsible to minister outside the corporate covering of a denomination.

That was certainly our anxiety. For example, we wondered how we would ordain young ministers. Without the visible succession to past ages that our denomination represented, what authority would we have to ordain anyone? How would we do missions work? Where would we find fellowship with other believers in other places? Although we knew other Christians in our area and other places, they were "not quite the same as we." We wondered how we would fit in, or whether we would even want to fit in.

Strangely enough, we might have never formed real relationships with other kinds of Christians had our former denomination not forced our hand. However, once we were no longer affiliated with the denomination, its members were discouraged from speaking in our church or from receiving us in theirs. This act of corporate shunning forced us to make new friends and alliances.

Of course, once we made those new friends, we had to confront our old prejudices (and the spiritual pride) that had kept us away from them to begin with. We soon discovered that those other believers did not believe (or behave) as we had been taught. The other Christians were, upon examination, as sincere and devoted to Christ as we.

What a revelation that was!

## What Replaces the Denomination?

Our denomination had increasingly characterized itself as "the authentic and restored New Testament Church." Those who left it soon often became anxious about finding the "REAL restored New Testament Church." Was the original Church more like the Baptists? Pentecostals? Churches of Christ? Presbyterians? What modern group looked the most like New Testament Christianity?

At Christ Church, we were trying to return to the most basics elements of our faith, what C.S. Lewis calls, "Mere Christianity." That had brought us face to face with the creeds.

The Apostles' Creed was something I had always heard about but didn't really know. Like most American Evangelicals, I felt that "creeds" and "confessions" were artificial statements made by people in the past who had no Bibles. Those who formed such statements probably meant well and did the best they could with what they had, but we now had the Bible. What possible use was a creed to a believer with a Bible?

Pat Gruits thought otherwise.

"Just learn it," she said. "You may not be more intelligent than the accumulated testimonies of centuries of Christians." She had already convinced our pastors - L.H Hardwick and Dennis Cagle - to use the Creed during the communion service long before I had joined the staff. So I thought I should go ahead and memorize it. After all, our children were learning it.

137

So I learned it. I then learned about it, what it meant, how it was written and how it was used in the early centuries of the church. I meditated on each line. I tried to think through all the implications.

I didn't discover anything in the Creed that caused me any real problems, (except perhaps the phrase "He descended into hell." Then I learned that it was perfectly kosher to translate it as "he descended to the realm of the dead.") As for "the communion of saints," I had experienced that reality since I was a child. We had always called the believers "saints" in West Virginia.

*But how could all of these people be Christian?*

So the Apostles' Creed was not an issue. However, the realization that nearly every Christian in the world claims to believe the doctrines of the Creed - even those who don't like creeds - that was a problem! How could they all profess to believe "mere Christianity" while worshipping so differently?

### Why Are There So Many Different Kinds of Christians?

I had taken advantage of my years in Montreal to visit non-Pentecostal churches. I went to a Coptic church, several types of Eastern Orthodox churches, Roman Catholic congregations and too many Protestant churches to count. In each one, I tried to talk to a church leader and then follow up my visit by reading books and articles about the denomination I had just visited. I had found formality and cold religious people in each, just as I expected. However, I had also discovered vibrant believers in each. But how could all of these people be Christian?

I had just assumed, I suppose, that Christian unity should manifest itself as something akin to "uniformity." In the beginning, I assumed, believers had thought and worshipped very similarly to the people of my little Pentecostal group. Then, shortly after the apostles, people claiming to be Christians had innovated and elaborated on the original themes until they had developed something quite different than what Christ had intended. As a result, we now had all these denominations.

That really did seem like a common sense explanation to me and I didn't really give it any more serious thought.

When one is a member of a denomination he often has an established spiritual identity. He does not usually feel responsible for inquiring about church history or biblical doctrine. Others have already settled those things. Every one of his friends is a member of the same denomination as he. Everyone he knows shares his presuppositions and his spiritual vocabulary. He doesn't ask questions about such things anymore than he would ask why he eats fried chicken while the Greeks across the street eat grape leaves. Were you to ask him about that, he might say, "Well, we eat fried chicken because that is what normal people eat; Greeks eat grape leaves because their ancestors came from a place where there was no fried chicken. When they become real Americans, they will learn better, bless their hearts."

There is such sweet innocence when one lives within as tight a community as we had experienced in our denomination.

Something happened to us though when we became pastors of an independent flock. Because our former denomination had made it impossible for us to maintain meaningful church relationships with our old friends (although we were able to keep a few personal friendships) we began to reexamine our identity. The questions about spiritual life that resulted were sometimes frightening, at least for me.

As we pondered these questions, hundreds and then thousands of people were rushing through our doors. For the most part, the new members of Christ Church did not share our denominational background. They came from every denomination imaginable. Most of them were tired of doctrinal issues anyway, so it was easy to ignore divisive issues for a while. However, we knew that the time would come when we would have to decide what to teach our children and new converts.

In the spring of 1987, Pastor Hardwick asked me to identify the beliefs that historic Protestant Christianity viewed as the core teaching of our faith. He gave me a set of Schaff's exposition of the <u>Creeds and Confessions of Christendom</u> and told me to summarize the books in a short paper.

We took that paper to a meeting we called with a group of people from our background in Chicago. For three days, we hammered out a statement of sixteen doctrinal beliefs that we thought would allow us to move forward. We called it "The Chicago Confession."

We had worded our statement to intentionally echo the great themes of historic Christianity. However, we also intended the statement to protect our specific emphasis on the Holy Spirit, which we felt had been long understated (and even ignored) by the great minds of Western Christendom.

In the following year or so, we were amazed as various adaptations of our doctrinal statement made their way across the country. Hundreds of Charismatic assemblies quickly adopted it as their own formal statement of faith.

Although the ground now felt a bit more solid under our feet, I was left with questions about Christian spirituality. Why did Christians worship so differently one from another? I had to know.

Once again, before studying the issue, I had supposed that all believers had once worshipped very simply. Someone prayed, someone read a passage, someone preached; then everyone went out to serve their communities. Worship was no more complicated than that. Then power-hungry church leaders forced elaborate systems of ritual that choked out the Spirit. My study revealed that although this view was not entirely off base, it was grossly overstated. The fact was, there had always been Christian liturgy, Bible teaching, and Charismatic gifts within the churches. None of our contemporary forms of Christianity were entirely foreign to earlier centuries of believers.

*Why did Christians worship so differently one from another?*

Why then had modern churches isolated their forms of worship one from another? And why did Christians tend to be so hostile toward one another when it came to their manner of worship?

My obsession to recover the *Real* New Testament church had moved me from a preoccupation about doctrine to one about worship and spirituality. I wanted to understand biblical worship and how it had developed through history.

One thing for sure, I was certain that I had experienced a New Testament encounter with the Holy Spirit. My Evangelical friends were mistaken in how they explained the worldview of the apostles and early Christians. The spirituality of the early believers was not like that of modern American Evangelicalism, nor like that of the Reformation,

141

for that matter. Although I believed the Reformers had substantially recovered New Testament theology, they had not recovered New Testament spirituality. On that matter at least, early Methodists and Pentecostals were closer in spirit to the spiritual culture found in the Book of Acts, the Epistles and the subsequent generations of early believers. Indeed, this point (in my opinion) has been made conclusively by the way in which Christianity has exploded lately in those parts of the globe we used to call "the third world."

Although Evangelical and Reformed critiques of Pentecostalism and the Charismatic movements are often deserved (and necessary), those critiques often lack an appropriate humility. Reformed Protestantism feels the freedom to critique Pentecostals; they do not tend to receive critique from Pentecostals. At any rate, the culture of European rationalism and the resulting suppression of intuition, spontaneity - indeed of the divine unpredictability of the Holy Spirit - just cannot be forced upon the practice and worldview of the early Christians. In that sense, I remained – and remain – a Pentecostal.

Nonetheless, early Christian worship was not a free-for-all. How could one even think such a thing after reading the elaborate depictions of Old Testament worship, accounts of how early Christian believers experienced such worship in the temple, the fact that many Jewish priests became believers, and that the Apostle John describes liturgical worship in heaven, many years after Pentecost?

Once again, Pat Gruits, Mrs. Pentecostal herself, insisted that sacramental life was not only compatible with our Pentecostal experience but that it expressed Pentecostal experience in ways mandated by scripture. There was a biblically mandated form for Christian spirituality, in other words. It had been handed down from New Testament times.

That form had been a loose adaptation of the Jewish Passover liturgy, and although it could become an "empty form," it was not the form itself that was at fault. "Vessels leak," she used to say. "They must be continually refilled."

As I studied further, it became obvious to me that this "form" had not been foreign to any believer until very recently. Roman Catholics had certainly elaborated the form with gestures and clothing, architecture and obscure theological explanations. The Presbyterians had simplified the rituals and reformed the theology that explained the form. Methodists had substituted grape juice for the wine. Baptists had replaced the chalice with shot glasses. However, underneath all this diversity was a single form, which appeared to me to have remained essentially consistent for 2,000 years.

When I finally encountered the written communion liturgy in the Book of Common Prayer, I was shocked to discover that it was not very different than the words my father had said over the communion table when I was a child. His words had been less formal, more "folksy," but were essentially the same form passed down through oral tradition from the past.

Of course, I had been reading C.S. Lewis. His book Mere Christianity had already convinced me that we were on the right track. He helped me understand that our people had come from every part of the Lord's church not only to receive, but to offer what they had learned in their journey of faith.

My struggles came to an end one Sunday evening as I prepared for church. I had been reading William Barclay's notes on Ephesians when I suddenly had a powerful urge to write. So I found a legal pad. I began to categorize the Christian churches according to how they worshipped under three columns: Liturgical, Evangelical, and Charismatic.

Under each of these columns, I wrote descriptive words about their historical origins: Temple, synagogue, and the prophetic tradition.

"Wow," I thought, "all forms of Christian worship had Jewish origins! We should not have been arguing these past few centuries about the 'pagan' elements of liturgical worship but rather about whether it was proper to maintain Old Testament forms in a New Testament era!"

I quickly added other descriptors: awe, understanding, and experience. These were the objectives of each form of Christian worship, I decided.

On a roll now, I added: Sacrament, Bible study, experience. These were the means by which God is met within these different expressions.

More terms followed: priest, rabbi, and prophet: these were the biblical models of ministry in the different churches.

Finally, I added the line that blew my mind and has never stopped amazing me: Father, Son and Holy Spirit: believers in each expression of Christian faith tend to prefer worship that direct them to God as they primarily view Him. The tri-unity of God is reflected in the tri-unity of His church!

| Worship Tradition | Liturgical | Evangelical | Pentecostal |
|---|---|---|---|
| Biblical source | temple | synagogue | prophetic |
| Central activities | sacrament | study | celebration |
| Mode of Worship | ceremony | exposition | spontaneity |
| Ministry model | priest | rabbi | prophet |
| Central concern | reverence | understanding | experience |
| Central focus | Father | Son | Holy Spirit |

The Muslims view God as "One without internal distinctions." Therefore, for them, unity necessarily implies uniformity. In Islam, a God without internal distinctions requires his people to eliminate internal distinctions from the congregation. In contrast, Christians worship a God whose Oneness flows from an internal dynamic within His nature. That dynamic involves difference and distinction and invokes difference and distinction in the worshippers.

*After a season with us, some return to a more clearly defined part of the Body of Christ.*

On the Day of Pentecost, Peter said this to the people of Jerusalem, "this Jesus, being by the right hand of God exalted, and having received from the Father the promise of the Holy Spirit, has poured forth this which you both see and hear." A God with internal distinctions inhabits a church with internal distinctions.

As a local church, we are spiritually and organically united with God's Church through all times and in all places. We therefore have a responsibility to reflect, in both our doctrine and our spiritual life, the love, power and glory of God in His fullness.

In other words, we must faithfully and capably teach the scriptures, embody sacramental life, and remain open to (indeed, continually invite) the power and presence of the Holy Spirit.

How this has worked out practically is this: Christ Church seems most comfortable to those who like living near the crossroads of Christianity. That is why people continue to come from every part of the church to worship, and even to make Christ Church their spiritual home. However, our church is not for everyone. Some prefer churches that are more predictably attached to a single stream of the church.

145

After a season with us, some return to a more clearly defined part of the Body of Christ.

I wrote The Emerging American Church to express the spiritual implications of what we had experienced here. When I wrote it, a convergence of Christian worship styles seemed foreign and threatening to many. However, in a few short years, the idea of "three streams of Christianity" became commonplace. Few younger church leaders today would view this idea as controversial. In their world, it just "is."

As the Christian revival in the Global South has continued, this is the form it has most often taken: rooted in history, committed to scripture and fervent in Spirit. For this reason, I believe the culture of Christ Church has prepared us for the expected 700,000 people who will be coming from all parts of the globe to our city in the coming decade. Although we honor our Southern Evangelical/Pentecostal roots, God has been gradually preparing us to catch the wave of 21st century Christian revival: a global church that reflects the fullness of Christian expression.

The three streams of Christianity converge in this church to form a mighty river of Christian history, contemporary relevance, and prophetic power.

# THE RIVER KEEPS FLOWING

Josh Lawson grew up in our church. In fact, he was a little boy when most of the events we have talked about in this book occurred. By the time he was ready for college, our congregation had gone through a number of traumatic events. As a result, the church had shifted into survival mode. However, as events in his life would soon demonstrate, the vision had been planted deep into the hearts of the next generation, despite the church's momentary distractions.

Josh went to Baylor in 2003, uncertain about what path his life should actually take. He knew he didn't want to join the party scene though; he wanted to find a way to make his life count. While in college, he became a part of a discipleship house and a church that only strengthened that desire.

As he was concluding his course of study, he became an intern at Christ Church. He had the good fortune to be assigned to the mentorship of Pastor Eric Falk.

So we must digress.

Anyone even loosely acquainted with Christ Church over the last few years will know about Eric, our missions pastor. He was one of those 'stealth saints' we talked about earlier. Highly intelligent, deeply spiritual, and terribly mischievous, he was humble almost to the point of self-effacement. Most people tended to underestimate his maturity and leadership qualities. When Montelle Hardwick was dying, I went to the hospital one day to just sit with her. I thought she was unconscious but at one point she stirred, looked at me and asked,

"Dan, are you watching Eric Falk?"

"I see him," I responded.

"He's a good one. Keep your eye on him."

I knew what she meant. She was thinking that he might be our next senior pastor. I had already thought that and fully intended to help him find the training he needed. He was a reluctant leader but already had the qualities of a man who would probably season into a wise and godly pastor.

*• • •*
*All that is left down here is the glow of glory where they once walked.*
*• • •*

Most people reading this know that Eric was tragically killed when the car he was driving hit a patch of black ice and was sent spinning into the path of oncoming traffic. He was headed to Waco, Texas, for a missions conference with a group from our church. Emmy Scott, a passenger in the car, was killed too. But I'm getting ahead of the story.

To be mentored by Eric is a passport into the hearts of our congregation. He and Emmy are the patron saints of our young adults, and as time passes, we have forgotten everything they ever did wrong or even human. All that is left down here is the glow of glory where they once walked.

Eric and Emmy were on their way to visit Josh that night. That's important to the story, as you will see.

"Eric talked about Christian life in a way that helped me envision church in a new way," Josh said. "He made me long for Christian community, a place of family where people help one another grow in God. We talked about pouring our lives into a small group of people who would have a heart for the nations and do whatever it takes for the Great Commission to be fulfilled.

He didn't know how to do it yet, but Eric had his focus on touching the world, and he made me want to do that too.

Christ Church wasn't quite ready to do that at the time and we both found that discouraging. So when I returned to Waco, I decided that I needed to move to Africa and become a monk."

(Jenny, Josh's wife laughs at this comment as she looks down into the face of her little infant boy. Josh had obviously not made a very good monk.)

"Yeah," she always laughs at that," Josh said.

"When I told my mom about my desire to sell everything and move to Africa to become a monk, she said that I needed to 'grow where I was planted.' That meant that I should stay there in Waco and plant my roots down deep until God gave me new direction. So that's what I did.

I joined Antioch Community Church because I saw that the people there really wanted what Eric and I had talked about. They formed community in small groups and discipled people with a heart for the nations. It was in community that I went deeper into my faith and learned how Christ uses His body to form us into disciples.

After meeting Lucy Pitkin, who worked for Christians Against Poverty in Bradford, England, I decided to form a not-for-profit corporation called Restoration Financial Ministry. I actually had been making good money in the insurance business but I had a zeal to help people get free from debt and from the materialism that pushed them into debt. That was great and all, except that I was getting married in five months and starting a ministry with no salary!

Fortunately, when I told her Dad about my crazy idea, he gently said that he trusted me and believed in me.

After a few months, we were actually beginning to get support. Then our senior pastor, Jimmy Seibert, asked me one day why I was starting a para-church organization. I thought he wanted to close our work down for a minute, but what he actually wanted was to pull my ministry into the local church because he believed that the local church should be taking the lead in seeing people financially restored. So that's what we did.

I decided to use Financial Peace University. I'm from Christ Church Nashville, right? That's what we do. But I thought FPU in our church needed facilitators who were able to give pastoral care to the people. FPU is a profoundly Christian program, but we wanted to put our roots deeper into scripture, point people towards eternity, and encourage people to find their personal calling.

Did I tell you that I interned with Dan Miller one time for several months?

Dan Miller talks about vocation all the time – the idea that everyone has a purpose and that joy comes from finding and living out that purpose.

We wanted to bring all that together in Waco.

In our first class, we had forty-two families. When we added up our accumulative amount of debt, it was over a million dollars. We suddenly realized that debt was a major issue in our church and it was actually preventing us from fulfilling God's purpose for our lives here in Waco and around the world. We now have a goal for everyone in our church to be debt free in the next 10 years. We also helped one another discover our calling. FPU is a great way to form small groups, as you know. However, you don't have to disband those groups just because the program is finished. The groups can go on and the facilitators can become real spiritual leaders of a flock. Not every facilitator feels called to that, but some do."

Josh's story really encourages me. It tells me that the vision God planted in our church long ago is still here.

A few weeks after I became the senior pastor, I wondered if I had done the right thing. I felt my age and thought about the wisdom of assuming the senior pastorate of a church at fifty-five. Then I thought about my assignment:

Raise up leaders,

Teach and practice the ancient future faith,

Build community, and

Reach the nations here and abroad.

I thought about our motto: Opening the soul to the presence of God.

It became clear to me that this pastorate was not about any new vision I might have. It was simply to recover the core culture and calling of the church.

*However, in retrospect, God has been preparing us for a long time for this hour.*

The world has changed since Loren Cunningham came. Nashville has become a cosmopolitan city with immigrants from around the world. Our church neighborhood is filled with new languages and faces. However, in retrospect, God has been preparing us for a long time for this hour.

## Josh Lawson's Vision

I'll finish this book by telling you about a vision Josh Lawson had. Let he and Jenny represent a new generation of leaders and perhaps his vision will encourage us with insight into what God is up to.

"When Eric Falk and Emmy Scott died, Jenny and I came to their funerals. After all, they had been traveling to Waco for our mission's conference. During Eric's funeral, I closed my eyes and I immediately saw a massive mountain. In

151

that mountain I could see there was a mighty river, swirling but without a way to get out. I zoomed out to see the outside of the mountain again and all of a sudden the river burst out of the side of it. The river began to flow into the valleys below and it brought new life, growth and greenery. I thought that mountain was Christ Church and I thought I heard God say, there are great resources (both people and money) in this church if only they would let that river run."

I was just concluding my work on this book when he told that story. He told it in a missions conference to a gathering of young adults. He had been too small to know about the sermon I had preached years ago, or about Loren Cunningham. He had no idea I was writing this book, or what the title was. But when I heard it, I felt the reaction around me. A congregation was saying "yes," just as they had twenty-five years ago.

So let it run. Let it run!